JEANNE KOHL JENKINS

....is presently an assistant professor of sociology and education at California State University, Long Beach; she also conducts workshops and lectures in women's studies and is a Title IX consultant to preschools and school districts.

PAM MACDONALD

....is an early childhood education and art specialist; she sets up and teaches open-option, non-sexist programs for children and adults.

They are both parents and are committed to the philosophy that growing up is an exciting adventure.

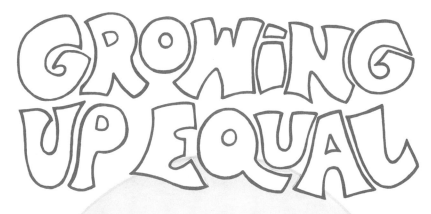

GROWING UP EQUAL

Activities
and resources
for parents
and teachers
of
young children

Jeanne Kohl Jenkins
Pam Macdonald

handlettered and illustrated by Pam Macdonald

PRENTICE-HALL, INC. Englewood Cliffs, New Jersey 07632

A SPECTRUM BOOK

Library of Congress Cataloging in Publication Data

JENKINS, JEANNE KOHL.
    Growing up equal.

    (A Spectrum Book)
    Bibliography: p.
    Includes index.
    1. Socialization. 2. Sex role. 3. Education,
Preschool. I. Macdonald, Pam, joint author. II. Ti-
tle.
HQ783.J44   301.41   78-16970
ISBN 0-13-367862-8
ISBN 0-13-367854-7 pbk.

Editorial/production supervision by Carol Smith
Text handlettered and illustrated by Pam Macdonald
Chapter openings and cover designed by Mona Mark
Manufacturing buyer: Cathie Lenard

A SPECTRUM BOOK

10 9 8 7 6 5 4 3 2 1

Printed in the United States of America

PRENTICE-HALL INTERNATIONAL, INC., *London*
PRENTICE-HALL OF AUSTRALIA PTY. LIMITED, *Sydney*
PRENTICE-HALL OF CANADA, LTD., *Toronto*
PRENTICE-HALL OF INDIA PRIVATE LIMITED, *New Delhi*
PRENTICE-HALL OF JAPAN, INC., *Tokyo*
PRENTICE-HALL OF SOUTHEAST ASIA PTE. LTD., *Singapore*
WHITEHALL BOOKS LIMITED, *Wellington, New Zealand*

❀❀ACKNOWLEDGMENTS❀❀❀

Special thanks to the people
who gave us permission to
reprint their materials.

Dominic Paul Cappello for his caricature sketches of
    the authors on page i.
Roni Shepherd for her illustrations on page 12.
ACTION FOR CHILDREN'S TELEVISION for excerpts used from
    ACT Guidelines and the television viewing statistics
    on pages 39 and 42.
Alfred A. Knopf, Inc. for the anecdote on the origin of the
    term "sandwich" on page 145, from LOVE AT FIRST BITE
    by Jane Cooper. (Copyright © 1977 by Jane Cooper).
Patti Johnson for her contributions to the "Aggression Cookies"
    recipe on page 97.
FREE TO BE FOUNDATION for the poem "Helping" by Shel
    Silverstein on page 115 (from FREE TO BE... YOU AND ME
    published by McGraw-Hill. Copyright © 1972, Ms. Foundation
    for Women, Inc.) and for the poem "My Dog Is a Plumber"
    by Dan Greenburg on page 191 (from FREE TO BE...YOU
    AND ME published by McGraw-Hill. Copyright © 1972
    Free To Be Foundation, Inc.).
Mabel Watts for her poem "Maytime" on page 155.
    (Copyright © 1954 by Humpty Dumpty, Inc.).
Bev Veitch for the recipes for "Sandwich Faces" and
    "Ironed Sandwich" on page 144 (from A CHILD'S COOKBOOK
    by Bev Veitch, Thelma Harms, Gerry Wallace and Tia
    Wallace).
D.G.P., a special friend, for the poems about trash on
    page 122.
Gandoff Zurcon for his poem about band aids on page 162.
Dustin Macdonald for his drawings on pages 19, 25, 96-98,
    169 and for his anecdote on page 169.

To our children

Randy
Brennan
Dustin
Terra
Kyle
Devon

who were the inspiration for our book and in whom we hope the message of the book will live on.

THANK YOU

While we worked very hard on this book (Thank you, Pam! Thank you, Jeanne!) many others helped in a variety of ways.

OUR VERY PERSONAL THANKS GO TO...

Our parents.....Virginia Davison Celotto and Elizabeth and Lloyd Kohl.....for setting the stage for our personal and educational efforts and achievements;

Ken Jenkins....for being the parental role model we have exemplified in GUE, the life-mate of Jeanne, and for sharing his scientific insight into the biological basis of sex differences;

Don Penkoff.....for giving Pam "space"..... in providing a hideaway in which to work as well as a shoulder to lean on;

Bill Macdonald.....for being "tender and tough"...and who during the writing of this book experienced the true meaning of non-sexist parenting.

AND, OUR THANKS FOR ASSISTING IN THE ACTUAL PREPARATION OF GUE GO TO.....

Roni Shepherd.....for sharing her artistic knowledge and up-front critiques as well as for introducing Pam to ball-park franks;

Jean Sinness and Elizabeth Kohl....for editing and typing drafts of GUE which helped immeasurably in our finishing on time;

Dustin Macdonald and the children of Peppermint Playhouse and of Mrs. Peters' 1977-78 Kindergarten class in Seal Beach, California...for contributing their free and innocent yet perceptive drawings;

Helen Pasley....for sharing her invaluable insight into children's feelings;

Patti and Loren Johnson....for critiquing GUE enthusiastically and objectively and for the slogan "better for both";

The staff at the Isabel Patterson Child Development Center at California State University, Long Beach....for sharing their open-option, non-sexist activities and resources with us;

Carol Smith, Jeannette Jacobs, and Lynne Lumsden of Spectrum Books, Prentice-Hall....for giving us editorial and artistic assistance and putting up with our faux päs. (Hang in there, Carol!)

AND, FOR SUPPORT IN OTHER WAYS...

The Surfside-Sunset Support Team.....for providing encouragement, "energy," and often needed and always appreciated "R and R" distractions;

Suzanne, Peter and Riana Guttridge....for giving Jeanne time to work by entertaining Terra.

AND LAST, BUT SO IMPORTANT,

A special thanks to each other....for giving one another a boost over each personal hurdle, for allowing needed "space" and preserving our close friendship through it all!

CONTENTS

Most of us appreciate variety... in foods, in clothing styles, in decor, in recreational activities, and in people. And, we like to believe we are unique and are not of the same mold as everyone else... a cookie that has been cut out by the same cookie cutter from the same dough and decorated with similar, if not the same, frosting and adornments.

Yet, many of us have not been fully aware that society has two basic cookie cutters ...one marked "feminine" and the other marked "masculine." These cookie cutters can also shape people into careers as well as personality types (as evident in the book I'M GLAD I'M A BOY, I'M GLAD I'M A GIRL by Whitney Darrow, Jr.). The following excerpts illustrate:

"Boys are doctors. Girls are nurses.
Boys invent things. Girls use what boys invent.
Boys are policemen. Girls are meter maids.
Boys are strong. Girls are graceful.
Boys are Presidents. Girls are First Ladies."

The message in this book, as in so many books for young children, is that boys and girls are totally different from one another. Boys grow up to do certain kinds of work and girls other kinds. Boys act one way; girls another way.

INTRODUCTION

While we concur that there are some differences—biological ones—we do not agree that these should govern career and/or activity choices. We believe that the examples from the book illustrate STEREOTYPES which are based on sex. These constrain and limit children during their formative years and consequently carry over to adulthood.

Many girls have the ability to become doctors but don't because they have never learned to perceive this role as an option for females. Many boys are graceful and have the talent to become dancers but do not because they have never learned to perceive this role as an option for males. Also, while many girls would like to be active and play in sports, they refrain as they have learned to perceive these as inappropriate for "young ladies." And many boys who are sensitive refrain from expressing their feelings for fear of being labeled a "sissy." These children are kept from exploring roles and behavior because they have been molded by societally determined masculine and feminine cookie cutters.

And, we all know how that affects ADULTS, too. We have ALL been affected by stereotyping and discrimination. Too many MALES have suffered from anxiety about their masculinity and from a higher incidence of...
● strokes ● heart disease ● ulcers
● early death ● poor self-concept
from constantly having to prove themselves superior in work ● athletics ● strength ● toughness ● dominance ● intelligence.
Too many FEMALES have suffered from...
● poorer jobs ● poorer pay ● poorer status ● over-dependence on others ● lack of self-confidence ● a security syndrome
and having to rely on appearance rather than on skills they could have developed.

MALES and FEMALES have both suffered from low self-esteem if they have not been able to measure up... if they haven't been strong and successful enough or sexy and beautiful enough.

YOU can help children avoid a lot of this by opening up their future world rather than by trying to SQUEEZE them into confining cookie cutters. If very young children see ALL future roles as open to them and if they are encouraged to learn a wide range of competencies ...in nurturing, cooking, cleaning, working with tools, fixing things, expressing feelings...then girls AND boys will benefit as adults...in their self-concepts, their jobs, and in their interpersonal relationships.

THUS, our book is all about what people who care for young children can do to reduce the imprint of these "cookie cutter" influences and to enable young children to be "decorated" in ways that enhance them as individuals, regardless of their sex.

THE PURPOSE OF THIS BOOK, then, is to provide a handbook for people...
- parents
- relatives
- preschool and primary teachers
- friends

...who would like some practical ideas for exposing young children to a wide range of activities and helping keep them from being locked into stereotypical feminine roles and masculine roles.

Specifically, OUR OBJECTIVES are to assist you in:

- creating a non-sexist, non-limiting environment for children;
- helping children to be individuals;
- providing equal exposure for children in understanding and learning skills related to future adult roles; and in
- helping children become less likely to stereotype and discriminate on the basis of sex—or anything else!

AND, very importantly,
- to have fun with children and to share new experiences with them.

goals objectives purpose

WAIT A MINUTE

Does this sound threatening to you? Are you getting a gnawing feeling in the pit of your stomach that is telling you that you don't want your son or any little boy to learn to be a girl or vice-versa?

If so, WE AGREE WITH YOU! And let us reassure you we are not advocating the reversing of the present situation. We do not want to bring up boys to be feminine or girls to be masculine What we do advocate is...

ANDROGYNY...

Definition:
Taking the best parts of femininity and masculinity and providing the opportunities for girls and boys to adopt those that interest them and those with which they feel comfortable.

If girls want to be active, learn to do carpentry work, as well as be gentle and able to express emotion...WONDERFUL! And, if boys want to do the same...TERRIFIC!

BETTER FOR BOTH

6

FEEL BETTER?

But are you still a little worried about the "price" these children might have to pay because of being a little different from some other children?

Are you wondering about a boy being ridiculed by others if he "cries" when he is upset or if he plays with dolls?

Are you worried about a girl being teased by others for not "acting like a lady" if she climbs trees or enjoys getting dirty?

GROWING UP ISN'T EASY even under the most ideal conditions. However, we believe that if children are reared in such a way that they feel comfortable with what they are doing and feel secure in knowing they are accepted by people who are important to them, they will be better equipped to handle life's demands.

YOU can help children develop values so they can appreciate and accept people as INDIVIDUALS rather than adhere to rigid expectations and stereotypes. You can help them cope with changing situations.

I AM AN INDIVIDUAL

NOW, WHAT IS GROWING UP EQUAL?

GROWING UP EQUAL consists of resources and activities for you to use in creating an open-option non-sexist environment and in helping children develop skills which will enable them to have greater opportunities to grow up equal with one another. Some of these are centered around child-adult participation and some solely around child participation.

Please do remember that we have included a great variety of activities which we strongly recommend your using with BOTH GIRLS AND BOYS. The objectives of the book cannot be met if certain activities are selected for use exclusively by boys while others are selected for use only by girls. We believe that when all activities are used, they will serve to provide children with REAL OPTIONS for their development and future as they will have been exposed to so many varied experiences.

Each chapter is comprised of special features. These will be recognizable to you by the following symbols:

PURPOSE OF THE CHAPTER

The introductory part of each chapter that specifies what we think is important about the chapter.

AWARENESS ACTIVITIES

The awareness-raising activities are for readers to do or think about. They will help make clear the mechanisms and consequences of sex role stereotyping and discrimination on our lives.

FACTS AND FIGURES

Pertinent facts and figures are included that we believe will be of interest and help you to understand the premises of the book.

RESOURCES

Resources can be obtained from libraries, book stores and companies. These are "extras" which you may use to "enrich" the activities or for your own information.

MENTAL HEALTH BREAKS

The "M.H.B.'s" are especially for YOU. They are fun things to think about or do during a "break" from child rearing.

INITIALS

Initials following some resources, e.g., ((C) indicate toy companies, distributors and non-traditional publishing companies. See pages 50, 51 and 61 for addresses.

Throughout each chapter we have given suggestions on organizing and implementing the activities. You may want to modify them, depending on the needs, interests, ages and ability levels of the children with whom you are interacting.

There is also space for you to jot down some of your reactions. At the end of the book is a page that can be torn out and sent to us with suggestions for additional activities that you may have found helpful in working with young children, as well as any changes you think we might make in the book.

ENJOY

GROWING UP   EQUAL

G.U.E.

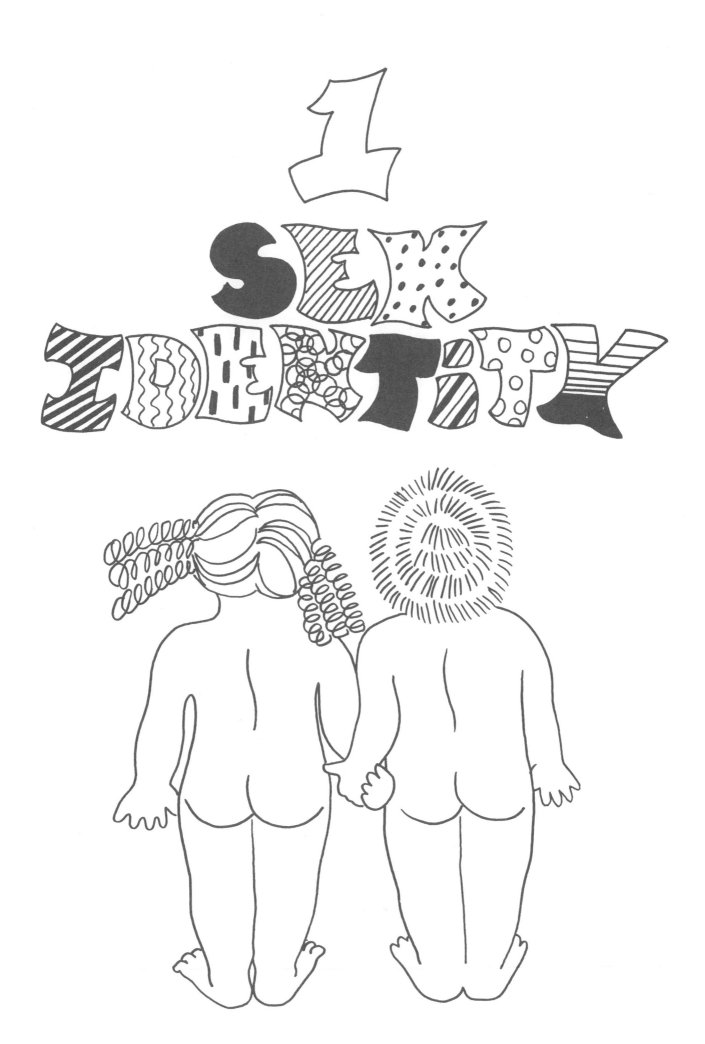

SEX IDENTITY

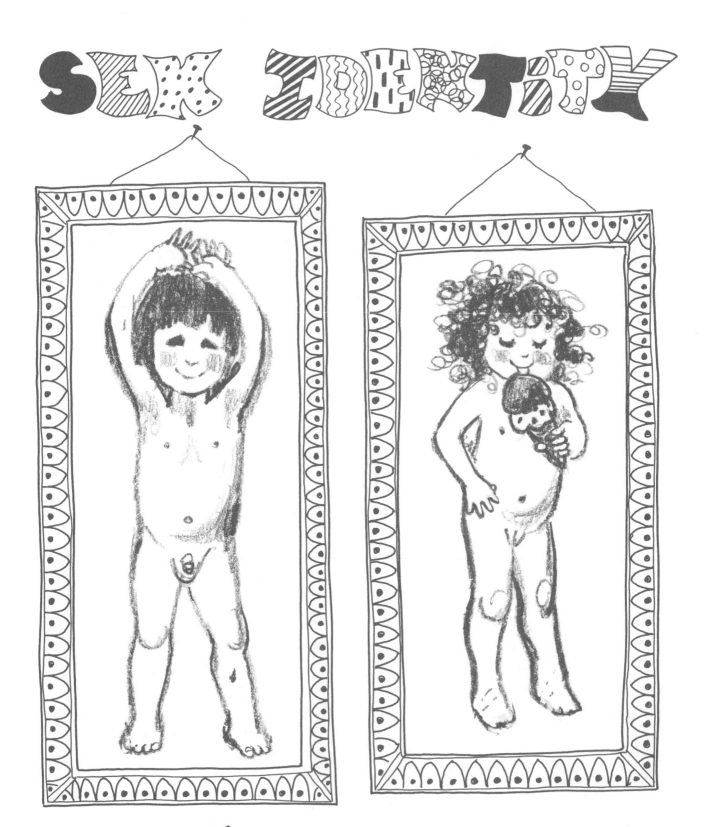

CHAPTER 1

WHO AM I

One of the most difficult and confusing concepts for a child to grasp is WHO she or he is and WHAT IS EXPECTED of her or him. Often children learn to associate their entire identity, as well as what they "should" and "can" do, with whether they are female or male. And, the preschool years seem to be the critical period for learning to define oneself as female or male.

WHY
The purposes of this chapter are to provide:

● an understanding of what sex identity is and how it is learned

● activities which can help preschoolers understand that they will always be of the same sex—male or female—but that this need not limit them.

DEFINITIONS

Confusion exists among scholars and the lay public regarding the terminology associated with sex and gender. Below are the definitions as we use them:

SEX: the biological condition of being female or male

GENDER: the psychological differentiation describing femininity and masculinity

GENDER IDENTITY: one's understanding of being male or female: I am a boy; I am a girl

SEX (OR GENDER) ROLES: behavioral and personality characteristics associated with being feminine or masculine; e.g., a female being feminine by being emotional and "playing the role" of a housewife or nurse; a male being masculine by being independent and "playing the role" of provider or doctor

SEX IDENTITY: one's internalization of the sex roles associated with being female or male. Sex identity is a girl's or woman's self concept of being feminine and of being biologically female; a boy's or man's self concept of being masculine and of being biologically male.

SEX

Young children as well as many adults often confuse maleness with masculinity and femaleness with femininity, i.e., they confuse biological sex with gender which is culturally acquired.

A boy is male because of biological distinctions, i.e., his anatomy and physiology, his having:
- x and y chromosomes, testicles, a penis and, as he gets older,
- a greater amount of facial hair
- a greater amount of testosterone
- the ability to produce sperm.

A girl is female because of biological distinctions, i.e., her anatomy and physiology, her having:
- x x chromosomes, a vagina, a clitoris, ovaries and, as she gets older,
- menstrual cycles
- the ability to bear children
- the ability to lactate
- a greater amount of estrogen.

These are BIOLOGICAL characteristics and are therefore innate or inherent to sex differences. They constitute maleness and femaleness.

BIOLOGICAL—GIRL—BOY

GENDER

FEMININITY and MASCULINITY, on the other hand, constitute gender and are psychological and behavioral characteristics that are culturally assigned and learned and have been traditionally viewed as influencing the ways in which people act as females and males. Masculinity and femininity are associated with and differentiated by:
- dressing styles / hair styles
- wearing of cosmetics
- types of occupations/careers
- physical activity
- demeanor
- personality characteristics
- child rearing

SEX IDENTITY

Unfortunately, many boys and men seem to think that they are not male unless they prove their masculinity by being tough, aggressive, strong, cool, independent and dominating. Likewise, many girls and women seem to think that they are not female unless they prove their femininity by being domestic, fragile, passive, weak, emotional, dependent and subordinate. Thus, the male who is artistic or who likes to work with small children may question his maleness and the female who is career-oriented or who is independent may question her femaleness.

These are misconceptions. A boy or man is male regardless of the extent to which he is masculine. A girl or woman is female regardless of the extent to which she is feminine.

We find it very sad, and very unnecessary, that anyone should suffer or question his/her sex identity because of societal norms governing masculinity and femininity.

this chapter deals with this concern!

We want to assist you in helping children understand that they are and always will be of the same sex to which they were born, no matter what they do or what they like. But, we also want to help them understand that all parts of them are equally as important as their being male or female.

In other words, we don't have to go to either extreme—to deny sex differences as being part of us (after all, we do have biological differences) or to maintain that they are everything, that being male or female is absolutely critical in determining what we can and should do.

The remainder of this chapter includes information concerning how children internalize their sex identity as well as activities and resources for you to use in helping children understand, but not be limited by, their sex identity.

HOW YOUNG CHILDREN SEE THEMSELVES

The early years are critical:
By three years of age, children know that they are a girl or a boy. (Kagan, 1969)
By 3-4 years of age, they know what people expect of them in terms of their behavior, preferences, and psychological characteristics. (Kohlberg, 1966)

Stoller, the Director of the Gender Identity Research Clinic at U.C.L.A., maintains that "core gender identity"— the sense of femaleness or maleness— is established in the first two or three years of life as a result of "the parents' conviction that their infant's assignment at birth to either the male or female sex is correct."

Everything that happens to the child during this time is gender influenced and provides for the child's learning of a particular sex role from then on.
(Stoller, 1967)

HOW IS SEX IDENTITY ACQUIRED?

While biological factors such as chromosomes, hormones, and anatomy can certainly play a part in determining how males and females behave, there is just too much evidence existing for socio-cultural influences as well.

1. Parental Perceptions

2. Contact with adult role models

3. Differential Treatment by Parents

4. Learned through the Culture

PARENTAL PERCEPTIONS

"Selective Perception"— parents "see" their newborns differently based on the sex of the baby:

Thirty pairs of first-time parents, one-half with new born daughters and one-half with new born sons, were asked within twenty-four hours of their child's birth to describe their new baby.
"Daughters, in contrast to sons, were rated as significantly softer, finer featured, littler, and more inattentive" even though there was not found to be an actual difference in size or weight between the male and female babies. (Rubin, et al., 1974)

CONTACT WITH ADULT ROLE MODELS

There are three major theories which attempt to explain how sex identity is learned.

 ## COGNITIVE-DEVELOPMENTAL THEORY:

The child learns through developmental stages by gradually thinking through what it means to be a male or female. The child adopts a sex identity which is reinforced by identification with the parent of the same sex.

 ## IDENTIFICATION THEORY:

The child learns through identification with the same-sex parent, although the boy initially identifies with his mother, but gradually his identification transfers over to his father, whom he sees as more powerful.

 ## SOCIAL-LEARNING THEORY:

The child learns through imitation and by being rewarded for exhibiting behavior consistent with her/his sex.

DIFFERENTIAL TREATMENT BY PARENTS

RESEARCH INDICATES:

- Starting at age six months, girls receive more physical contact and are talked to more than are boys.
- Fathers display affection more with girls.
- Girls learn to rely more on the opinion of others.
  - Parents are more likely to accept clinging, dependent behavior from girls.
  - Parents respond more to boys' large muscle movements.
- Boys are encouraged not to cry while girls usually receive support for doing so.
- Boys and girls are given different kinds of toys: girls' focusing on nurturing and domestic skills and boys' on career skills and muscle development.
- Girls learn to be more concerned with their appearance-they are usually not allowed to get dirty but are supported in being perfect in grooming, thus inhibiting active playing.
- Boys learn to be more concerned with their physical prowess-fathers roughhouse with them and teach them sport skills.
- Parents encourage boys to solve their own problems, while they more often help girls solve theirs.
- Parents are more protective of their girls.
- Parents encourage their boys to be more independent than they do with their girls.
- Parents are more tolerant of assertiveness and physical aggression in their boys than in their girls.
- Mothers sanction boys negatively for imitating their ways (such as in domestic activities) while encouraging girls.

Parents are more likely to tolerate girls' acting in sex-inappropriate ways (like being "tomboys") than they are boys' (like being "sissies").

Usually boys are not clearly told what they should do as males, rather what they should not do. They are more likely than are girls to be threatened, punished, and have anger directed toward them if they do not live up to parental expectations of "masculinity."

 All this seems to induce "sex-role anxiety" in boys and a consequential "overstraining to be masculine, in virtual panic of being caught doing anything traditionally defined as feminine, and in hostility toward anything even hinting at femininity, including females themselves." (Hartley, 1974)

 Is this what most parents would want for their sons if they were really aware of the implications of their actions? Hardly.

A FASCINATING, THOUGH TRAGIC, STUDY!
One of a pair of identical male twins lost his penis as a result of a mistake during electro-cautery circumcision of his penis. After consultation with and assurance from physicians that the child would be able to "differentiate a female gender identity in agreement with her sex of rearing," the parents decided to bring up the child as a female. Plastic surgery would be performed to construct female genitalia and hormonal treatment would be done at the time of adolescence.
RESULTS so far: two children, identical genetically and hormonally, who at the age of ten have become very different in terms of sex identity. According to the mother, the "boy" is masculine, messy, copies his father, likes and excels at sports, and rejects homework. The "girl" is tidy, imitates her mother, likes pretty dresses and plays with dolls. Certainly, though a tragic occurrence, it is one which clearly demonstrates the LEARNING of sex identity, femininity and sex roles. (Money and Ehrhardt, 1975)

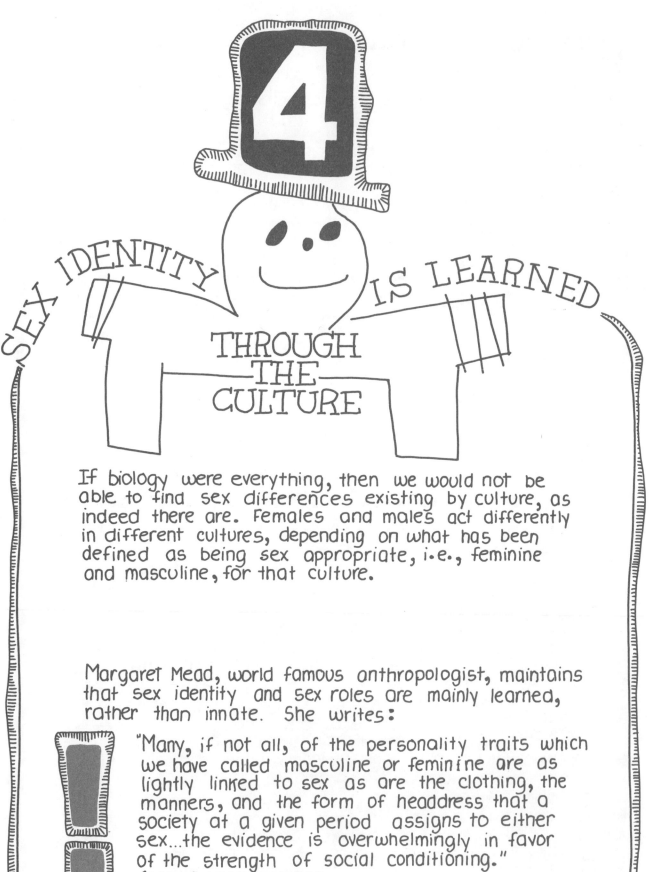

4

SEX IDENTITY IS LEARNED

THROUGH THE CULTURE

If biology were everything, then we would not be able to find sex differences existing by culture, as indeed there are. Females and males act differently in different cultures, depending on what has been defined as being sex appropriate, i.e., feminine and masculine, for that culture.

Margaret Mead, world famous anthropologist, maintains that sex identity and sex roles are mainly learned, rather than innate. She writes:

"Many, if not all, of the personality traits which we have called masculine or feminine are as lightly linked to sex as are the clothing, the manners, and the form of headdress that a society at a given period assigns to either sex...the evidence is overwhelmingly in favor of the strength of social conditioning."
(Mead, 1969, p. 260)

STEREOTYPES

Culture influences the learning of sex roles and sex identity by perpetuating sex-role stereotypes, such as that boys are always strong and girls are always neat.

DEFINITION

Stereotypes: overgeneralizations concerning expectations about "sex-appropriate" activities, abilities, attributes, and preferences

SEX-ROLE STEREOTYPES

Sex-role stereotypes reinforce sex identity. They dictate what people should be like based on sex and thus limit and channel children into prescribed roles which consequently affect their sex identities.

Young children use stereotypes in distinguishing between males and females. Children are able to tell females from males by the age of four. (Kohlberg, 1966)

But they usually use social, rather than biological, criteria to make this distinction, such as with clothing, shoes, occupations. Occasionally they use an accurate biological criterion, such as "Men can't have babies."

The younger the child (apart from infancy and toddlerhood) the more rigid is the adherence to sex-role stereotypes.

To a young girl/boy, to be a girl is to be feminine; to be a boy is to be masculine. They do not usually have the sophistication necessary to distinguish between actual femaleness or maleness and the culturally learned expectations of sex identity—femininity or masculinity.

AWARENESS ACTIVITIES

1. Think of all stereotypes which YOU, as an adult, hold about females' having to be "feminine" and males' having to be "masculine." Do these hold true for ALL females you know? For ALL males you know?

2. Ask children what girls and women are like; what boys and men are like. What stereotypes do they hold?

3. Discuss with them the possibility of non-stereotyped roles. Show or talk about examples of people they know who are in non-stereotyped roles.

4. Read Chapter 2 on becoming aware of influences on sex identity.

Harwood (1975) interviewed 48 3-5 year old children to determine at which age preschool children acquire rigid sex-role stereotypes. RESULTS: 4-and 5-year-old children had begun to form more rigid sex-role stereotypes. 3-year-old children still show flexible sex-role concepts.

5. Try using Harwood's questionnaire with your child(ren):
Can a boy play with a doll?
Can a girl play with a truck?
Can a woman be a doctor?
Can a woman be a dentist?
Can a man be a nurse?
Can a woman be a firefighter?
Can men be teachers?
Can women be police officers?
Can men be cooks?
What would you like to be when you grow up?

6. Observe your child(ren) and, if possible, other children for sex-role differences.
- Is there a difference between female and male behavior, emotional responses, preferences, abilities, and/or attributes?
- Does age make a difference?
- Do girls act differently when they are with boys and vice versa or when they are in mixed-sex groups?
- Do children adhere to traditional expectations for their sex?
- Do they live up to the stereotypes?
  - Do they stereotype other children by sex?
  - How do other people (friends, parents, relatives, other children) channel your child into conventional roles- by word or by action?
- How does your child respond?

Two children, age 4, were sitting beside each other in preschool. Tim was not sitting as motionless as Jenny. Finally, she leaned toward him and said, "Why don't you sit up like a lady?" He was too stunned to reply!

HERE ARE SOME STEREOTYPES ASSOCIATED WITH PRESCHOOL CHILDREN

boys will
be boys
roughhouse
big boys
don't cry!

cars • hammers • saws

building • power

plays team sports • muscles • running

doctor • house of energy • the "dirty" word

higher achievement expectations

uniforms • plays outdoor

very loud • firefighter

hates to comb hair

companion dolls have "action" clothes

likes toys that encourage manipulation

construction

plays tag • collects bugs • splashes in mud

monsters and quicksand

wrestles to prove strength

climbing trees • wants fast shoes

"spiderman"

DO YOU WANT YOUR CHILD TO FIT INTO THE MOLD?

ladies first
play house
mommy's
little helper

fairy princess
it's not nice to hit
clean
wants to please
likes to help
dreams
walks
reads
girl's play house alone
wants to be a mommy
companion dolls have apron and kitchen utensils
graceful
baby dolls
sewing machine
glamour dolls: spend time and money on clothes and make up
"look so pretty today"
jump rope and hopscotch
toy iron
needs things fixed
passive, watching
Cinderella
cries easily
smiles alot
flirtatious with men

your preschooler

Write the characteristics along the dotted lines which describe your son's/daughter's individuality.

How does your son/daughter fit into this preschool cookie cutter?

28

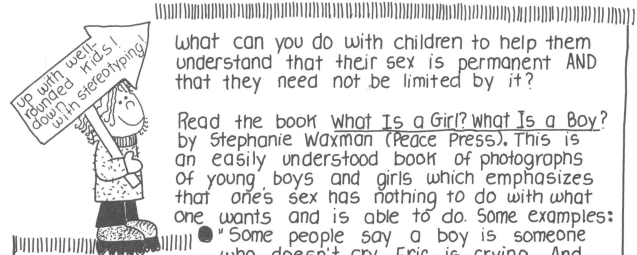

What can you do with children to help them understand that their sex is permanent AND that they need not be limited by it?

Read the book <u>What Is a Girl? What Is a Boy?</u> by Stephanie Waxman (Peace Press). This is an easily understood book of photographs of young boys and girls which emphasizes that one's sex has nothing to do with what one wants and is able to do. Some examples:

● "Some people say a boy is someone who doesn't cry. Eric is crying. And he's a boy."
● "If a baby is a girl, she will always be a girl."
● "A boy is someone with a penis."
● "A girl is someone with a vagina."

In conjunction with, or independent of, the book, have your child(ren):
● Draw in the body parts on an outline of a body that you have drawn. Do the same for both sexes.
● Draw his or her own body (for older preschoolers) and name the parts of the body.
● Form her or his body in clay or Playdoh.

Also read and discuss the book <u>Bodies</u> by Barbara Brenner (E.P. Dutton), which includes photographs of boys' and girls' bodies in the nude and doing different things.

Discuss the permeability of one's sex and that a girl need not fear losing her vagina (or gaining a penis) or becoming a boy if she plays with boys OR a boy need not fear losing his penis (or gaining a vagina) or becoming a girl if he plays with girls.

Read <u>You, How Your Body Works</u> by Leslie McGuire (Platt-Munk).

If you prefer that your preschooler NOT be molded by this cookie cutter, then go on to the next chapter and find specifics on........ ..... HOW children are molded and WHAT you can do to counteract traditional influences.

2

INFLUENCES

1. ROLE MODEL
2.
3.
4.
5. THE ADVENTURES OF SUPER KID
6.

CHAPTER 2

As discussed in Chapter 1, children have a very clear idea of their own sex role by the time they are three to four years old! Girls and boys DO and DON'T DO certain things because they view them as being appropriate for one sex rather than for the other or for both sexes. HOW DOES IT HAPPEN that they have these ideas?

Children learn sex roles from a variety of sources. Young children are not as sophisticated as adults in discerning what is REAL rather than MAKE-BELIEVE, and what is DISTORTED and/or EXAGGERATED, and accordingly they perceive sex role stereotypes as truth and reality. However, most of what is presented to them regarding sex roles IS distorted and/or exaggerated.

Specifically, what we are referring to and what is detailed in this chapter are the influences on preschool children of role models found in:

PEOPLE
TELEVISION
TOYS
DOLLS
BOOKS
SCHOOL

 WHY The purposes of this chapter are
• to raise your awareness of the varied influences on children's understandings of sex roles
• to provide activities and resources to use in changing sex-role stereotyping by exposing children to non-sexist role modeling and other influences.

We believe this is important so that girls and boys see alternatives and options!

PEOPLE

WHO was important to you as a role model when you were a young child? why? what did you learn from her/him?

ROLE MODELS. Role models are people who play an important part in shaping our feelings about ourselves AND what we do and will do. Our self image and behavior involve our sex role identity. Girls look to adult women, boys to adult men; and by doing so LEARN what they think they should be doing as females or as males.

ROLE MODELING?

PARENTS

The most obvious role models for children are parents. Girls are encouraged to be like "Mommy" and boys like "Daddy." Besides learning feminine and masculine personality characteristics, children receive vocational guidance in the traditional family; eg., girls learn to value the domestic and nurturing roles and boys the breadwinning roles. BUT, whether or not parents serve as traditional role models, they can influence their child(ren) in non-sexist ways.

Make an inventory of what you (and your spouse) do as role models. As a woman, do you solely engage in domestic and nurturing roles? As a man, do you limit your activities in the home to those involving yard maintenance, repairs and/or disciplining?

If you don't already, TRY performing in some non-traditional roles for your sex so that your child(ren) can see you as multifaceted and capable in many diverse areas as well as learning that it is "all right" for women to do_____ and/or men to do_____.
Some suggestions for:
   WOMEN_____ wash car, drive the family car on family outings, mow lawn, clean garage, hang pictures, watch a sports event on T.V., pay for meal when the family eats out, repair something, others....
   MEN_____ plan menu for week, change diapers, arrange flowers in a vase, take care of sick child, clean house, fix breakfast and send children off to school, read bed time story to child, others....

OTHER ROLE MODELS

Other role models exist besides parents, such as relatives, babysitters, friends, neighbors, doctors, librarians, preschool teachers, local store owners, etc. LIST the role models who you believe are important influences on your child(ren)'s understanding of sex roles.
ROLE MODEL_____ INFLUENCE_____
Is one sex prevalent over the other in terms of: AMOUNT of influence? QUALITY of influence? To whom else could you expose your child(ren) to broaden perspectives and options and his/her attitudes?

35

PARENTING MANUALS can have a great

influence in guiding parental role modeling behavior. While many current manuals stress a sharing of roles, many still encourage parents to act in certain ways based on their being a mother or father as well as to behave differently with sons than with daughters. For example, Dodson (1976) writes that "Father has a crucial role.... sons.... physical interaction and roughhousing; daughters...... encourage her coquettishness and femininity."

FATHERJOURNAL   by David Steinberg
NON-SEXIST CHILD RAISING   by Carrie Carmichael
FATHER FEELINGS   by Elliot A. Daley
TENDERNESS IS STRENGTH   by Harold C. Lyon Jr
THE WHOLE BABY CATALOG   by Cathy Roberts Ross and
    Denise Marie Begg
RIGHT FROM THE START: A GUIDE TO NONSEXIST CHILD REARING
    by Selma Greenberg
HOW TO RAISE INDEPENDENT AND PROFESSIONALLY SUCCESSFUL
    DAUGHTERS   by Rita Dunn and Kenneth Dunn
WHO WILL RAISE THE CHILDREN, NEW OPTIONS FOR FATHERS (AND MOTHERS)
    by James A. Levine
PARENTS' YELLOW PAGES by Princeton Center for Infancy

* The above books are annotated in Chapter 6, Child Care Section

NON-SEXIST LANGUAGE

As a role model yourself, be especially careful of your language (and we're not referring to 'cussin')! English is a sexist language (as are most languages). Think of alternative ways of saying things.

In a 1974 study of sexist language in the Random House Dictionary, the sampling of words was found to include:
- 68% masculine gender words
- 23% feminine gender words
- 9% masculine or feminine words.

MASCULINE GENDER words connotated achievement, ambition, aggression, competitiveness, competence, dominance and intelligence.

FEMININE GENDER words connotated weakness, incompetence, submissiveness, dependency, and timidity. (Gershung, 1974)

EXAMPLES

free children
super kid
child (ren)
boy / girl

boy and girl	preschooler
mankind	human race
man power	human energy
manhood	adulthood
brotherhood	personhood
he and she	s/he, he/she, or she/he
him and her	him/her, her/him, or them
men	humans, people
mankind	human race
man made	synthetic, manufactured
workman	worker
____ man team	____ player team
police man	police officer
chairman	chair person
fire man	fire fighter
mail man	mail carrier

T.V.

TELEVISION has a very powerful influence on young children. Research has shown that not only does television distort children's perceptions of reality (e.g., children are apt to perceive police and doctors as monopolizing careers) but also serves to suggest appropriate roles for males and females. Also, children spend an amazing amount of time being passive while watching T.V., which takes away from active participation.

IT'S A FACT!

In a 1970 study of "Sesame Street" (which is a very positive T.V. program in most respects) the ratio of males and females was 2:1. (Vogel, et al, 1970) In 1974, after "Sesame Street" producers had been notified by parents of concern over disproportionate ratio, the ratio was found to be 2.5:1. WORSE! Also, the male-dominated segments comprised 75% of the total viewing time. The two women in the show are not actively employed. (Bernabei, 1974)

WARNING: T.V. has been found to be harmful to your child's health.

Children under five years of age watch an average of 25½ hours of T.V. a week. By the time a child finishes high school, s/he will have spent 15,000 hours watching T.V. S/he will have been exposed to 20,000 commercials each year! (ACT, 1978)

T.V. CAN

- damage the ear drum
- dull the senses
- hurt the eyes
- stifle creative imagination
- become your child(ren)'s principal socializing agent outside of yourself and
- instill an attitude of spectatorship, and more.

YOU CAN

- Use television to help your child(ren) turn into television critics so that they will become aware that the children, men and women they see on T.V. are unrealistic and you can help them become wiser consumers.

IF YOU LET IT!

DO IT!

ADULT T.V. GAME

AWARENESS ACTIVITIES

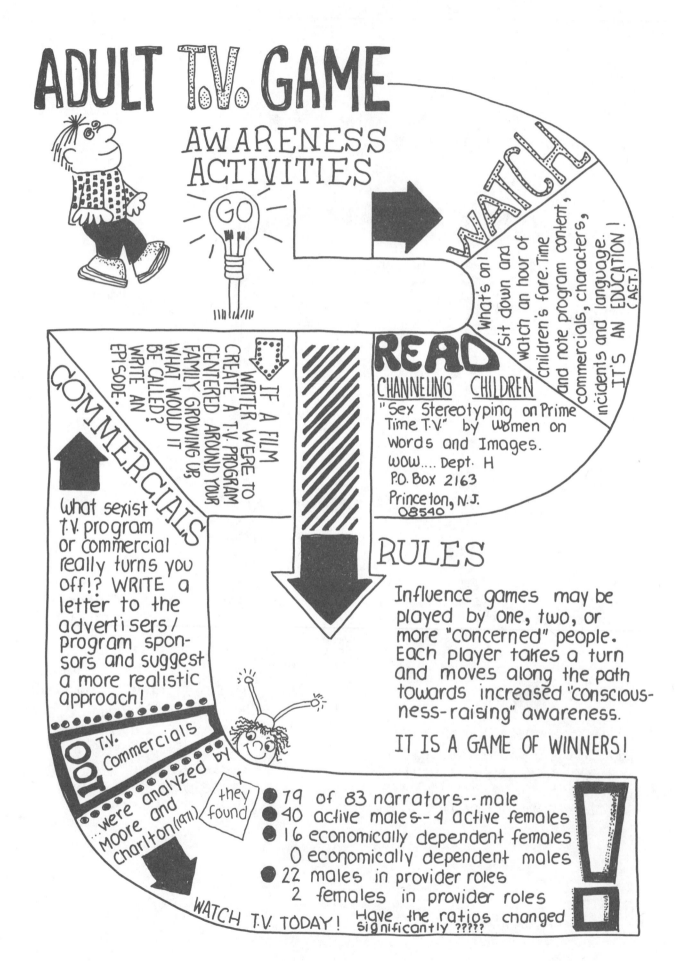

GO

WATCH

What's on! Sit down and watch an hour of children's fare. Time and note program content, commercials, characters, incidents and language. IT'S AN EDUCATION! (ACT.)

READ

CHANNELING CHILDREN

"Sex Stereotyping on Prime Time T.V." by Women on Words and Images.
WOW.... Dept. H
P.O. Box 2163
Princeton, N.J.
08540

IF A FILM WRITER WE'RE TO CREATE A T.V. PROGRAM CENTERED AROUND YOUR FAMILY GROWING UP, WHAT WOULD IT BE CALLED? WRITE AN EPISODE.

COMMERCIALS

What sexist T.V. program or commercial really turns you off!? WRITE a letter to the advertisers/program sponsors and suggest a more realistic approach!

100 T.V. Commercials ...were analyzed by Moore and Charlton (1971)

they found

RULES

Influence games may be played by one, two, or more "concerned" people. Each player takes a turn and moves along the path towards increased "consciousness-raising" awareness.

IT IS A GAME OF WINNERS!

● 79 of 83 narrators--male
● 40 active males-- 4 active females
● 16 economically dependent females
   O economically dependent males
● 22 males in provider roles
   2 females in provider roles

!

WATCH T.V. TODAY! Have the ratios changed significantly ?????

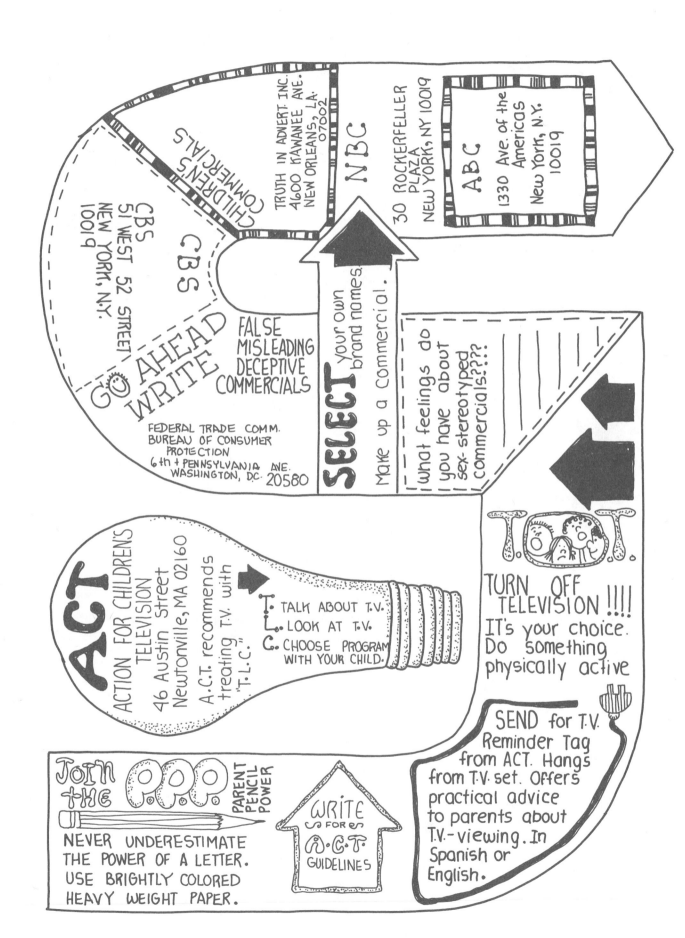

CHILDREN'S COMMERCIALS

TRUTH IN ADVERT. INC.
4600 KAWANEE AVE.
NEW ORLEANS, LA.
07602

NBC
30 ROCKERFELLER PLAZA
NEW YORK, NY 10019

ABC
1330 Ave. of the Americas
New York, N.Y.
10019

CBS
51 WEST 52 STREET
NEW YORK, N.Y.
10019

GO AHEAD WRITE

FALSE MISLEADING DECEPTIVE COMMERCIALS

FEDERAL TRADE COMM.
BUREAU OF CONSUMER PROTECTION
6th + PENNSYLVANIA AVE.
WASHINGTON, D.C. 20580

SELECT your own brand names.

Make up a commercial.

What feelings do you have about sex-stereotyped commercials????

T.O.T.

TURN OFF TELEVISION !!!!
IT's your choice.
Do something physically active

ACT
ACTION FOR CHILDREN'S TELEVISION
46 Austin Street
Newtonville, MA 02160
A.C.T. recommends treating T.V. with "T.L.C."

T. TALK ABOUT T.V.
L. LOOK AT T.V.
C. CHOOSE PROGRAM WITH YOUR CHILD.

SEND for T.V. Reminder Tag from ACT. Hangs from T.V. set. Offers practical advice to parents about T.V.-viewing. In Spanish or English.

Join the P.P.P.
PARENT PENCIL POWER

NEVER UNDERESTIMATE THE POWER OF A LETTER. USE BRIGHTLY COLORED HEAVY WEIGHT PAPER.

WRITE FOR A.C.T. GUIDELINES

CHILDREN'S T.V. GAME

AWARENESS ACTIVITIES

GUIDE

WATCH

Saturday morning T.V. with your child.

Read THE FAMILY'S GUIDE TO CHILDREN'S TELEVISION by Evelyn Kaye

NOTICE how females and males are portrayed on the programs as well as the commercials. WHAT types of products are boys/girls encouraged to want? NOTICE which programs portray "open" roles.

TAKE **10** BIG STEPS BACK AND SIT. T.V. CAN HURT YOUR EYES AND WHAT ABOUT POSSIBLE RADIATION? BONUS: TURN T.V. OFF

RULES

This children's T.V. Influence Game is most effective when enjoyed TOGETHER. (one, two, or more preschoolers and "concerned" adult(s)

IT IS A GAME OF WINNERS!

OPEN ROLES

TAKE A LEAP FORWARD ...for WATCHING
- Zoom
- Mr. Rogers
- Blue Marble
- Sesame Street
- Shazzam and Isis

AND DISCUSSING STEREOTYPIC AND OPEN OPTION T.V.

S.O.S. STAMP OUT SEXISM

A.C.T. Guidelines
- Look out for TV behavior your child might imitate.
- Look for TV characters who care about others.
- Look for women who are competent in a variety of jobs.
- Talk about the differences between make believe and real life.

FACTS

1) that two categories of products are presented and geared towards women:

1. Beauty aid and underwear supports, which emphasize females' need for male approval.

2. Domestic housekeeping aids, which emphasize females' compulsiveness regarding cleanliness and the inadequacy of those who are not immaculate housekeepers and fabulous cooks.

2) the commercials with whom s/he interacts daily. Help your child become more aware of the images that are stereotyped by the tube.

Nash (1975) found

$

While you are watching T.V. COMPARE the men/women s/he sees in adults with whom your preschooler(s)

COMMERCIALS

By the time your child is 18 years old s/he will have watched approximately 350,000 commercials. (Dunn and Dunn, 1977)

GO to the friendly grocer's shelves. Note the NAMES of household products. TALK about why such names are used.

WISE CONSUMER

HAVE YOUR CHILD make two piles of toys... one T.V advertised, the other more durable or her/his favorite toys. COMPARE FOR:
- quality
- interest level
- breakability

TURN OFF
- pop popcorn
- visit a friend
- chase butterflies
- practice tying shoe laces
- play charades
- pretend....day dream
- other?...

TOYS

Most children play with toys, whether they are expensive or handmade, new or hand-me-downs, or adapted from what is available around the home. Toys are important to young children. They provide entertainment, recreation, company and means for developing skills and knowledge.

In a sense, they are the "work" tools of young children. Toys also have a considerable influence on the learning of sex roles. While there are many sex-neutral toys—those okay for both boys and girls—MOST are for either girls or boys. AND children learn very quickly which are which!

One only has to take a quick survey of toys used by children in the home, in the preschool, in ads on T.V., in magazines, and in toy catalogs to see with what types of toys boys are encouraged to play as compared with girls. In general, girls play with toys involving nurturing and domesticity; they play housekeeper and mother. Boys play with toys involving physical manipulation, construction, power and careers; they play workers and strong men.

IT'S A FACT!

 In a 1975 study of toys used by 100 children, aged one to six years old...

GIRLS HAD MORE... dolls, doll houses, domestic toys... and their rooms were decorated with floral furnishings.

BOYS HAD MORE... vehicles, sports equipment, toy animals... and rooms were decorated with animal motifs.

On the average, the number of toys found in preschool children's rooms: one year old... 28 toys, six years old... 91 toys. No girls' rooms contained a single wagon, bus, boat, kiddie car, motorcycle, etc., of which 36 were found in boys' rooms. (Rheingold and Cook, 1975)

If you are an "average" family, you will spend $85 per child per year on toys. (Toy Manufactures of America, 1976)

Glancing through a 1977 Sears Christmas catalog we found:
- 99 female dolls, 17 male dolls
- 14 boys, 6 girls riding toys
- 11 girls, 1 boy using housekeeping/cooking toys

Toy manufacturers make more money by selling separate girls' and boys' toys than they would if only one set of toys were purchased by a family with both girls and boys. A good and expensive example of this is with girls' and boys' bicycles.

TOY

AWARENESS ACTIVITIES

GAME

WRITE FOR A CATALOG......

LEARN ME, INC.
642 GRAND AVE.
ST. PAUL, MINN. 55105
...books, puzzles, records, games... evaluated for quality and the absence of stereotypes.

TOYS THAT CARE
P.O. BOX 81
BRIARCLIFF MANOR,
N.Y. 10510
...records, anatomically correct dolls, sex education materials, puzzles, career dress up, non sexist, multi-ethnic.

LOOK through a store or mail order catalog for stereotyping. HOW are toys labeled as appropriate for girls, for boys? NOTICE the packaging!

CATALOGS

WHAT KINDS OF TOYS ARE DESIGNATED AS BEING FOR GIRLS _ _ _ _ _ _ _ _

_ _ _ _ _ _ _ _

BOYS _ _ _ _ _ _ _ _

_ _ _ _ _ _ _ _

READ

THE MAGIC HAT (LP)
K. WESTSMITH

children played happily together until there was a fence put up between the "boy toys" and "girl toys."

draw

A PICTURE BOOK WITH YOUR PRESCHOOLER. SOME TOPICS TO "DRAW" ABOUT
- your child(ren)'s favorite toys
- three wishes for gift toys
- rhyming words with toys
- an alphabet book of your child's toys.* CHECK FOR SEX TYPING OF THE TOYS.

HOW TO MAKE A BOOK: Staple typing paper between a piece of folded construction paper or old wall paper. Or thin poster board...

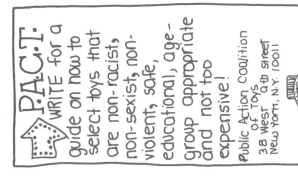

 WATCH

FOR THESE THINGS WHEN SELECTING TOYS...

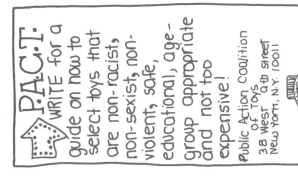

P.A.C.T.: WRITE for a guide on how to select toys that are non-racist, non-sexist, non-violent, safe, educational, age-group appropriate and not too expensive!

Public Action Coalition of Toys
38 West 9th Street
New York, N.Y. 10011

- safe
- durable
- fun
- provides non-sexist, multi-ethnic role models
- respectful of a child's intellect, self-esteem and creativity
  - non-racist and non-sexist in the way it is packaged, conceived and planned for play.
  - avoid toys that equate the accumulation of material goods with self-concept

TALK WITH **CHILDREN** ABOUT

1. MESSAGES THE BEST-ENJOYED TOYS ARE SENDING
2. CATEGORIES THAT ARE MISSING
3. PRODUCTION: WHICH TOYS ARE HANDMADE? STORE PURCHASED?
4. POPULARITY: WHICH ARE USED THE MOST? WHY?

BONUS **ACTIVITY**

It's time to see what messages your child(ren)'s toys are sending. On the day you decide to update-reorganize-throw out and/or categorize your child's toys OR want to do a mutual involvement awareness activity to discover how multidirectional or one-sided the toy chest is.... TRY THIS → During the pickup/put away time, separate toys into categories. Write down the number of toys in each category.

- books
- games
- nurturing toys, e.g. stuffed animal, doll
- self-operating or wind up
- old toys-that-still-look new (definitely a message here)
- other?
- records
- active toys, e.g. ball

NON-SEXIST TOYS

NAME OPTION TOYS IN YOUR CHILD'S TOY CHEST

WHAT GIFT DID YOU LAST GIVE A PRESCHOOLER?

OPEN OPTION? SEX STEREO-TYPIC?

WE CAN WIN

TOYS
NATURAL•NON-SEXIST•NEUTRAL

Toys nourish a child's imagination. They act as props for dramas the child works out in fantasy and practices in play. Children do NEED, ENJOY, and LEARN from toys. In Growing Up Equal, a child will be exposed to a variety of toys and not be restrained from using a given toy because it has been reserved "traditionally" for children of the other sex.

There are many toys that are "neutral" and "non-sexist" and have been used by both girls and boys. We encourage you to provide some of these toys for your child as well as some specific non-sex-role traditional types of toys to break down sex role stereotyping. Also, some toys are important even though they have a picture of one sex on the package. Children don't have to see the packaging, but DO write the toy manufacturer of your concern.

"NATURAL"

- the totally "unstructured" toy... sand, water, mud, snow, rain, trees, hills, grass, etc.

"NEUTRAL"

- children's back pack.... to carry goodies, travel treasures, snacks, etc.
- dress up clothes.... include "all" the accessories
- giant and/or regular size tinkertoys (Questor Educ. Products)
- chalk board, colored chalk, eraser
- large preschool size wood blocks. assorted sizes & shapes
- puppets.... stick, finger, small hand, Muppet, etc.
- drum and other musical instruments....if you're daring
- toy tent or large blanket
- handiperson's tools ..... garden tools
- play money.... cash register
- bathtub toys.... eg. Bathtubbies (Tomy)
- puzzles.... non-sexist ones
- ABC blocks.... wood, plastic, foam
- early-years camera, 2 shutter speeds & 3 distance settings
- bean bags, finger paints, hats, magnifying glass, toy telephone, large rubber ball and others

TOYS
NON-SEXIST

Recognize that not every toy, book, etc., LABELED "non-sexist, creative, educational, for all ages" is necessarily of high quality materials. we need to move beyond labels.

EXAMPLES:

- "Carrot-parent" (PP) non-sexist (neutral) parent in pink or cinnamon
- "Free to Be You and Me" by Marlo Thomas and Friends. (Bell Records) record to accompany book of same name.
- Occupational Puzzles (JP) female pilot, with male co-pilot, doctor, telephone linesperson, judge, lawyer, and garage mechanic
- Super Speed Racer (Fisher-Price) sexually-ambiguous driver (girl on one side, boy on other side) in 7-inch racing car
- Records and/or Cassettes with Matching Books (Caedom)- distributed through CBMC) HURRAY FOR CAPTAIN JANE, JELLYBEANS FOR BREAKFAST, IRA SLEEPS OVER, MARTIN'S FATHER, MY MOMMY IS A DOCTOR, THE SUNFLOWER GARDEN.
- Community Career Flannel Board (WAA) 27 male and female figures
- Wannabees (Gabriel) career skills play people with new options: male and female farmers, woman doctor and cow girl... include accessories.
- Dressing and Undressing Puzzle (CC) boy and girl with genitals shown
- Play Scenes Lotto (MB) multi-racial girls and boys in a variety of play scenes

Additional toys can be found throughout the book under particular subject headings. Distributors' addresses can be found on pages 50 and 51.

TOY COMPANIES AND DISTRIBUTORS

The following addresses are for writing to obtain catalogs and/or toys OR to express concern about toy packaging and advertising. *Those that appear committed to providing non-stereotypic toys for both girls and boys.

Avalon Industries (A)
Toy Craft Division
95 Lorimer Street
Brooklyn, NY 11206

* Childcraft Education Corp.
20 Kilmer Rd.   (CC)
Edison, NJ 08817

* Child Guidance (CG)
Questor Toys
Bronx, NY   10472

* Children's Book and
Music Center (CBMC)
5373 W. Pico Blvd.
Los Angeles, CA 90019

Creative Playthings (C)
Edinburg Road
Cranbury, NJ 08512

Dick Blick   (D)
P.O. Box 1267
Galesburg, IL 61401

* Freemountain Toys (FM)
23 Main Street
Bristol, VT 05443

* Fun-da-mentals (F)
Box 263
South Pasadena, CA 91030

Hastbro Industries, Inc. (HI)
Pawtucket, RI 02861
(Romper Room Toys)

Ideal Toy Corp. (I)
Hollis, NY 11423

Imco Toy Company, Inc. (ITC)
New York, NY
(Walt Disney Products)

*Judy Puzzles (JP)
312 North Second Street
Minneapolis, MINN 55401

Kenner Toys (K)
Box 789
Minneapolis, MINN 55460

*Learn Me, Inc. (LM)
542 Grand Ave.
St. Paul, MINN 55105

Mallet and Peg Shop
P.O. Box 90
Woodbury, CT 06798
(wood toy vehicles)

Mattel (M)
2 Penn Plaza
New York, NY 10001

Milton Bradley (MB)
Springfield, MASS 01101
(distributed by WAA)

Nova Educational Toy
and Equipment Co.
124 W. 24th Street
New York, NY 10011

*Pinky Puppets
271 Outlook Drive
Pittsburgh, PA 15228

Play and Learn Products
2298 Grissom Drive
St. Louis, MO 63141
(vehicles)

Playskool (P)
Milton Bradley
Chicago, IL 60651

Stone Mountain
Educational Projects
Roaring Brook Farm
Conway, MA 01341

*Toys That Care (TTC)
P.O. Box 81
Briarcliff Manor, NY 10510

*Women's Action Alliance (WAA)
370 Lexington Ave.
New York, NY 10017

INITIALS ( ) ARE FOR LOCATING COMPANIES'
RESOURCES THROUGHOUT GROWING UP EQUAL.

DOLLS

Dolls are miniature representations of people. Children, regardless of sex, race, ethnicity or social class, interact with dolls during their preschool years.

But most frequently it is the girl alone who is encouraged to play with dolls. Boys are often restrained from playing with them, even though they, too, can become parents as adults and can enjoy a companion doll.

The importance of dolls to child rearing is in the enormous variety of activities and behavior that they elicit FROM A CHILD. They represent the varied relationships that can be established with people, as motivated by the different types of dolls, such as the:

- baby doll
- companion doll
- ornamental doll
- ethnic doll
- glamour doll
- action doll
- military doll
- super-hero doll
- storybook doll
- paper doll.

doll POWER

LOOK AT WHAT DOLLS ARE PROVIDING FOR YOUR CHILD:
- develop values... how we perceive ourselves
- provide a friend/companion
- provide aesthetic sense
- strengthen a child's own and other's racial and cultural identity and understanding
- provide opportunities to role play
- provide opportunities to be nurturant and express emotions.

In a study of a Sears catalog, there were more dolls and their paraphernalia than any other toys. Sociologist Alice Rossi once remarked, "..... a girl may spend more years playing with her dolls than a mother spends with her children." (Rossi, 1964)

Beware of two types of dolls that are a powerful force in transmitting certain values to our children.

THE GLAMOUR DOLL... miniature replica of a fully developed woman, who spends alot of money on clothes and makeup.

THE ACTION DOLL... daring, rugged, and a "man's man."

These dolls are unquestionably two of the most popular types of dolls after the age of five— popular because they depict what a child thinks s/he wants to be as a grown-up. THINK of the values that are being projected... high fashion, beautiful body, dream house, violence, etc.

These are not necessarily negative, but they pose a problem if they are the only types of dolls a child has. The problem is that sex-stereotyped dolls allow only ONE option for adulthood.

TWO RECOMMENDED DOLLS

Preschoolers develop specific relationships with specific dolls. Usually they have two basic dolls: A COMPANION DOLL, perceived as a peer; and A BABY DOLL, viewed as a dependent personality.

The companion doll is a child's first doll and appears around the twos. The two-year-old is still in a solitary play stage and his/her companion doll helps facilitate awareness of personalities outside him/her self. The child is learning the concept of a "friend"... someone with whom to talk, eat lunch, share a secret, etc.

MAKE A LIFE-SIZE COMPANION DOLL

Take two pairs of old tights. Stuff with old nylons or pillow stuffing. Sew tights together at the waists—one pair will be the legs the other pair the arms. For the head, cut one leg from a pair of nylons ...stuff and sew securely between the arms.

Here's where the fun begins. Let your preschooler dress the life-size doll in his/her clothes. Provide a varied selection from your child's wardrobe, include hats, gloves, jewelry, etc. Create a face with buttons, felt scraps, yarn, etc.

Your preschooler will have a "friend" with whom to dance, talk, dress and undress, share, and experiment and experience with "people" interactions.

BABY DOLL

Around the mid-threes, because of increased activity in role modeling and dramatic play, children begin role playing "the parent." The baby doll is then incorporated into play as the pre-schooler's own child. The child is beginning to form nurturing skills... learning to provide for, protect and care for others, AS WELL AS the child care skills necessary for parenting. (See Living Skills chapter, Child Care.)

Both the companion doll and the baby doll are crucial in child rearing for they teach a child that s/he WILL NEED others (companion doll) and BE NEEDED by others (baby doll).

RESOURCES

- Archie Bunker's Grandson
- Baby Brother Tender Love, black or white skin (M)
- Brother and Sister Dolls- anatomically correct (CC)
- Daddy and Baby Beans, loving father doll with baby doll (M)
- Sasha dolls- include ethnic and male dolls (G)
- Mooks: 22-inch cloth dolls with anatomical detail (Erica Dodenhoff, 25 Bruceville Rd., High Falls, NY)
- Hand-sewn anatomically correct "minority" dolls- Black, Native American, etc. (CBMC)
- Celebration-of-the Clitoris dolls- hand sewn, fact sheet for parent- dialogue by Montessori teacher. (Doris Vine Conklin, Box 332, Talmadge, CA 95481)
- Pregnant Monkey Sock Doll- baby monkey can attach to breast (Monkey Business, Rt. 3, Box 153A, Celina, TENN 38551)

BOOKS

Books are an important source of pleasure and learning for preschoolers. Preschool picture books hold the interest of the young child as well as facilitate enjoyment without adult assistance. However, books also convey impressions to young children of the world and of sex roles. These impressions rarely parallel reality; the inherent contradictions are rarely explained to children, so they go on internalizing what they are seeing as accurate and true.

"androgyny"
..........taking the best parts...........

 Of the award-winning Caldecott books (best illustrated picture book of each year) from 1967-1971, the ratio of male to female in illustrations was 11 to 1......... when taking into account pictures of animals. (Weitzman et al., 1971)

 Besides including more males than females, which clearly contradicts reality, preschool picture books also depict sex-role stereotypes.

● mothers are exclusively at home; fathers exclusively work outside the home.
● girls are weak, clumsy, fraidy cats, tattletales and cry all the time.
● boys are tough, strong and never cry.

These books can be confusing for children who continually see pictures of mother at home if their mothers work outside the home;

OR for boys who do feel afraid at times;

OR for girls who do not tattletale or enjoy cleaning house.

Books also serve as motivators for future career choices. For example, in Weitzman's study, two twin Golden Books indicated what boys and girls can be: (both books by Walley)

WHAT BOYS CAN BE

fireman
baseball player
bus driver
policeman
cowboy
doctor
sailor
pilot
clown
zoo keeper
astronaut
president

WHAT GIRLS CAN BE

nurse
stewardess
ballerina
candy shop owner
model
star
secretary
teacher in a nursery school
bride
housewife
mother

NOTICE THE DIFFERENCES

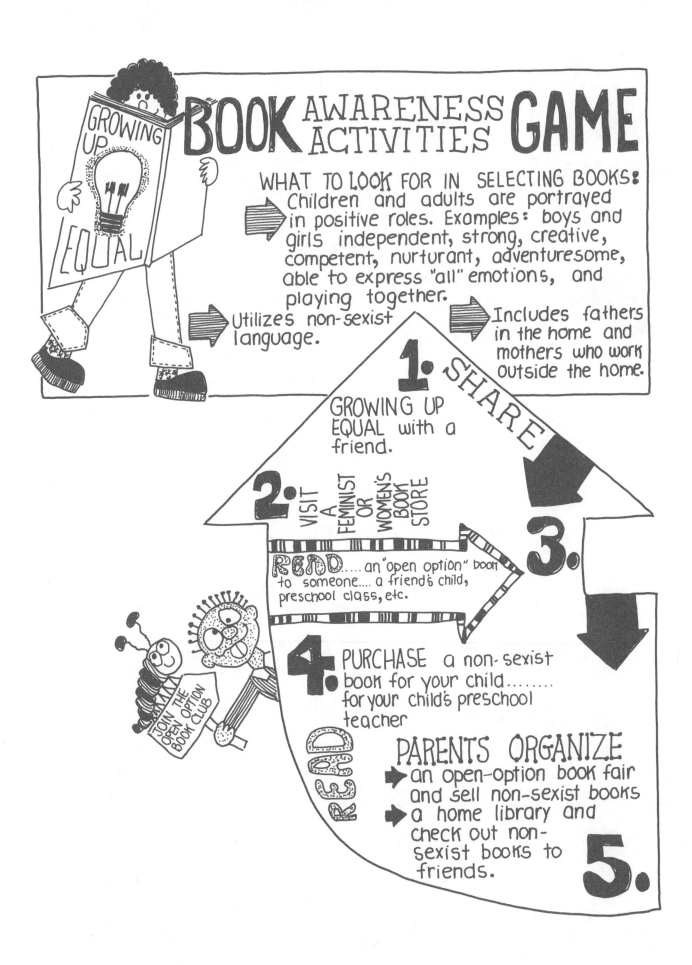

BOOK AWARENESS ACTIVITIES GAME

WHAT TO LOOK FOR IN SELECTING BOOKS:

➡ Children and adults are portrayed in positive roles. Examples: boys and girls independent, strong, creative, competent, nurturant, adventuresome, able to express "all" emotions, and playing together.

➡ Utilizes non-sexist language.

➡ Includes fathers in the home and mothers who work outside the home.

1. SHARE GROWING UP EQUAL with a friend.

2. VISIT A FEMINIST OR WOMEN'S BOOK STORE

3. READ..... an "open option" book to someone.... a friend's child, preschool class, etc.

4. PURCHASE a non-sexist book for your child........ for your child's preschool teacher

5. PARENTS ORGANIZE
➡ an open-option book fair and sell non-sexist books
➡ a home library and check out non-sexist books to friends.

JOIN THE OPEN OPTION BOOK CLUB

VISIT THE LIBRARY

CHECK OUT AT LEAST 10 EARLY CHILDHOOD BOOKS

1. Are the children and/or adults portrayed realistically? stereotypically?
2. How often are boys/men shown being passive, tender, crying?
3. How often are girls/women shown being clever, active, capable, brave?
4. What kinds of jobs are adult women and men shown doing?
5. What do you think children might learn from seeing these portrayals?

JOIN
THE FEMINISTS BOOK CLUB
2083 Westwood Blvd.
Los Angeles, Ca. 90025

WRITE
A NON SEXIST STORY. CHILD DICTATES.... ADULT PRINTS IT.... CHILD ILLUSTRATES.

SEND FOR A CATALOG FROM
AN OPEN-OPTION BOOK PUBLISHER

TRY THIS
IF SOME OF YOUR FAVORITE CHILDREN'S BOOKS ARE HEAVILY LADEN WITH STEREOTYPED STANDARDS OF BEHAVIOR.....

- Read she instead of he or vice versa when stereotypes appear.
- Discuss the stereotyped behavior and help her/him become a critical thinker.
- To increase children's character identification, try substituting your child's name in the place of one of the central characters - male or female
- Change sexist language.

STEREOTYPES ARE A BORE

REWRITE
a sexist nursery rhyme, such as "Little Miss Muffet" inviting the spider to join her for a picnic lunch. OR a fairy tale such as "Little Red Riding Hood" Outwitting the wolf and the wolf admitting at the end, "Little girls aren't as easy to fool as they used to be" or "They surely don't make little girls like they used to!" ANDROGYNOUS BOOK.....WORM...→

CHILDREN'S BOOK COUNCIL
175 Fifth Avenue
New York, NY 10010

Write for information on publishers of non-sexist books.

BIBLIOGRAPHY OF NON-SEXIST PICTURE BOOKS (FP) edited by Jeanne Bracken and Sharon Wigutoff

CHILDREN ARE PEOPLE by Judith Brunger-Dhuyvetter, P.O. Box 2428, Stanford, CA 94305 Annotated bibliography of non-sexist children's books.

CHILDREN'S LITERATURE: AN ISSUES APPROACH by Masha Kabakow

CHILD'S PLAY 226 Atlantic Ave., Brooklyn, New York, NY 11201 Catalog of non-sexist children's books.

A GUIDE TO NON-SEXIST CHILDREN'S BOOKS by Judith Adell and Hilary Klein, Academy Press Ltd. 360 N. Michigan Avenue, Chicago, IL 60601 Annotated bibliography.

LITTLE MISS MUFFET FIGHTS BACK by Feminists on Children's Media (FBM) A bibliography of non-sexist childrens books.

THE NEW WOMEN'S SURVIVAL SOURCE BOOK edited by Kirsten Grimstad and Susan Rennie Resource catalog.

RACISM & SEXISM CENTER FOR EDUCATORS Council on Interracial Books for Children, 1841 Broadway, New York, NY 10023 Write for informational pamphlet.

THE NATURAL CHILD Dept. 1578, 591 Rockport Dr., Sunnyvale, CA 94087 A comprehensive guide to non-sexist toys, books and records.

NON-SEXIST BOOK PUBLISHERS AND DISTRIBUTORS

Write for free book listings.
Send for catalogs.
Visit a feminists'/women's book store.
See the appendix for listings of feminist book stores.

Initials are for you to use in locating companies' resources throughout G.U.E.

AOS... All OF US, INC., Rte. 2, Box 128, Monmouth, ORE.
BWS... BEFORE WE ARE SIX, 15 King St. N., Waterloo, Ontario
CWEP... CANADIAN WOMEN'S EDUCATIONAL PRESS, 280 Bloor St. West, Toronto, Ont. Canada
CBMC... CHILDREN'S BOOK AND MUSIC CENTER 5373 Pico Blvd., Los Angeles, CA 90019
CP... ChinaBERRY PRESS, P.O. Box 7301, Tyler, TX 75711
FBM... The FEMINIST BOOK MART, P.O. Box 149, Whitestone, NY 11357
FP... THE FEMINIST PRESS, SUNY/College at Old Westbury, Box 334, Old Westbury, NY 11568
FREE... FEMINIST RESOURCES FOR EQUAL EDUCATION, P.O. Box 185, Saxonville Sta., Framington, MASS 01701
FTF... FIRST THINGS FIRST, 23 Seventh St., S.E., Washington, D.C. 20002
ICWP... IOWA CITY WOMEN'S PRESS, 116½ E. Benton St, Iowa City, IO 52240
IP... IMPACT PUBLISHERS, P.O. BOX 1094, San Luis Obispo, CA 93406
JWP... JOYFUL WORLD PRESS, 478 Belvedere St., San Francisco, CA. 94117
KCP... KIDS CAN PRESS, 830 Bathurst, Toronto, Ont, Canada, (BOOK PEOPLE in U.S. 2940 Seventh St., Berkeley, CA 94710)
KI... KNOW, INC.... P.O. BOX 86031, Pittsburgh, PA 15221
LM... LEARN ME, INC., 642 Grand Ave., St. Paul, MINN. 55105
LP... LOLLIPOP POWER, INC., P.O. Box 1171, Chapel Hill, NC 27514
NEFP... NEW ENGLAND FREE PRESS, 60 Union Square, Somerville, MASS 02143
NSP... New Seed Press, P.O. Box 3016, Stanford, CA 94305
PPI... PEACE PRESS, INC., 3828 Willat Ave., Culver City, CA 90230
RI... RAINBOW INSTITUTE, Box 13907, UCSB, Santa Barbara, CA 93107
SPI... SCARECROW PRESS, INC., 52 Liberty St., Metuchen, NJ 08840
TC... THE TWO CONTINENTS PUBLISHING GROUP, 30 E. 42nd St. NY, NY 10017
WMCLC... WOMEN'S MOVEMENT CHILDREN'S LITERATURE COOPERATIVE, LTD. P.O. Box 119, Mooroolbark, 3138, Victoria, Australia
WP... WREN PUBLISHING PTY. LTD., (order from WMCLC)
WRPC... WRITERS AND READERS PUBLISHING COOPERATIVE, (order from TC)

CHILDREN'S BOOKS

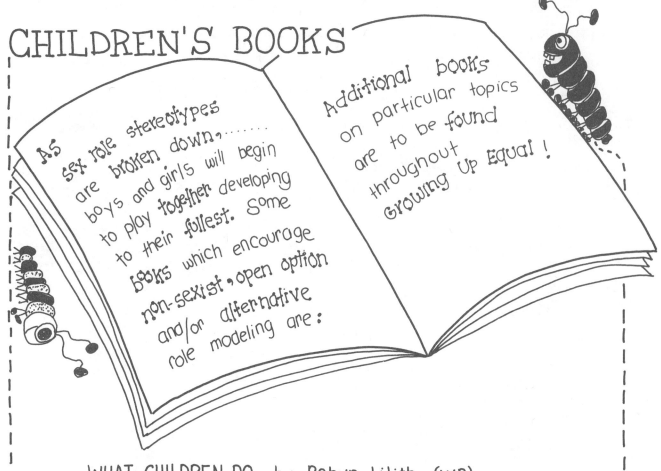

As sex role stereotypes are broken down,........ boys and girls will begin to play together developing to their fullest. Some books which encourage non-sexist, open option and/or alternative role modeling are:

Additional books on particular topics are to be found throughout Growing Up Equal !

WHAT CHILDREN DO by Robyn Lilith (WP)
Book of photographs in which children (names do not suggest sex) play together in a variety of activities.

A HOLE TO DIG by Ruth Krauss
First book of definitions with boys and girls doing everything together.

JOSHUA'S DAY by Sandra Syrowiecki (LP)
Story of a young boy's experiences in a multi-ethnic liberated day care center.

NOISY NANCY NORRIS by Lou Ann Gaeddert
Nancy is inventive and noisy.

FINDERS KEEPERS by Alix Shulman
Lisa, the best finder in the playground, invents a finders keepers game to play with friends.

JO, FLO, AND YOLANDA by Carole de Poix (LP)
Triplets are very different in their interests and abilities.

AMELIA MIXED THE MUSTARD AND OTHER POEMS
   by Evaline Ness Poems about unconventional girls
   and dedicated to "females all: big, little and middle."

AND I MEAN IT, STANLEY by Crosby Bonsall
   Presents a story about an active and imaginative
   young girl and a giant dog named Stanley.

THINGS WE LIKE TO DO by Evelyn M. Andre
   Girls and boys are pictured in a variety of activities
   such as baking cakes and playing with dolls and friends.

THE WINTER WEDDING by Robert Walker
   Girls and boys share non-competitive friendships
   at preschool.

GLADYS TOLD ME TO MEET HER HERE by Marjorie Weinman
   Irving and Gladys are best friends and play together.

THE CHRISTMAS CAT by Efner Tudor Holmes
   A story about a nurturing man, a lost cat and
   two boys on a Vermont farm.

LUCKY WILMA by Wendy Kindred.
   Presents alternative family styles while showing
   how Wilma and her dad discover how to be together
   on their weekends.

A TRAIN FOR JANE by Norma Klein (FP)
   Jane still wants a train for Christmas even though
   everyone around her suggests stereotyped ideas.
   (record and cassette available—see Toy Section)

MADELINE AND ERMADELLO by Tim Wynne-Jones (BWS)
   An imaginative girl creates a lively, interesting
   imaginary friend.

And, get and use the following dictionary which
   includes non-sexist definitions and
   illustrations with equal sex representation.
   AMERICAN HERITAGE SCHOOl
   DICTIONARY— Houghton Mifflin.
   (American Heritage Publishing Co., Inc.
   551 Fifth Avenue, N.Y., NY 10017)

SCHOOL

Many preschoolers attend some type of "school"...... a nursery school, a religious school, neighborhood co-op, a university sponsored child development center, etc.

Wouldn't it be frustrating if after all the time and effort that you have undoubtedly spent in helping your child develop a non-sexist attitude, your child were to be placed into a sexist and limiting environment when entering "school." Thus, we have included an observation checklist for your use.

- Inventory your own expectations, behavior and environment.
- Visit the childcare facility you would like your child(ren) to attend.
- Check for the equality of opportunity and treatment of children AND the presence of new role models rather than stereotypic examples.

Open-option child Care center

Checklizt

what to look for:

→ the environment

✓ non-sexist bulletin boards and other displays
✓ integrated groupings
  • seating arrangements
  • free play areas
  • eating areas

→ the children

✓ play together
✓ do not stereotype or discriminate (or, if they do, the teacher works to overcome these behaviors)

→ the teacher and aides

✓ both males and females
✓ treatment of girls and boys
  • warm and affectionate to both
  • encourages both to be independent, active and to express their emotions
  • encourages boys and girls to play together
✓ uses non-sexist language
✓ uses non-sexist discipline (doesn't differentiate between boys and girls)
✓ uses non-sexist requests for assistance (girls can also carry and lift; boys can also clean up)
✓ intervenes when children stereotype and/or discriminate against other children. ("You can't play in the kitchen .... you're a boy;" or "You can't play with trucks.... you're a girl.")

→ activities

✓ Are all areas available to, and utilized by, girls/boys?
  • housekeeping
  • block area
  • dress up area
  • carpentry area
  • sand box
  • bicycle area
  • ball/jumprope area
  • other

→ materials, toys, equipment

✓ Are all available to, and utilized by, both girls and boys?
  • blocks
  • records
  • games
  • puzzles
  • clothing in dress-up area
  • dolls and doll furniture
  • housekeeping equipment
  • trucks
  • musical instruments
✓ Is there an adequate quantity of non-sexist toys and books?

Resources and Books

➡️ DAY CARE AND CHILD DEVELOPMENT COUNCIL OF AMERICA, INC. 1401 K. Street NW, Washington, D.C. 20005

➡️ RESOURCE CENTER ON SEX ROLES IN EDUCATION
1156 Fifteenth St., Washington, D.C. 20005

➡️ "THE SOONER THE BETTER" (WAA)
Film on non-sexist education for young children

A MODEL FOR NON-SEXIST CHILD DEVELOPMENT (WAA)
Resources and bibliography for a preschool program.

AND JILL CAME TUMBLING AFTER: SEXISM IN AMERICAN EDUCATION
edited by Judith Stacey, Susan Bire, and Joan Daniels.
Selected articles on most aspects and levels of education.

LIBERATING YOUNG CHILDREN FROM SEX ROLES   (NEFP)
by Phyllis Taube Greenleaf.   An important guide centering
around non-sexist preschools.

NON-SEXIST EDUCATION FOR YOUNG CHILDREN (WAA) by Barbara Sprung.
A practical guide for teachers and parents.

PERSPECTIVES ON NON-SEXIST EARLY CHILDHOOD EDUCATION (WAA)
edited by Barbara Sprung.
Includes presentations made at the first National Conference
on Non-Sexist Early Childhood Education, October, 1976.

RESOURCES FOR CREATIVE TEACHING IN EARLY CHILDHOOD EDUCATION
(LM) Cultural awareness without sex or ethnic stereotyping.

SEXISM IN SCHOOL AND SOCIETY by Nancy Frazier and Myra Sudker.
A good overview for educators.

UNDOING SEX STEREOTYPES by Marcia Guttentag and Helen Bray.
A practical guide for educators.

UNLEARNING THE LIE: SEXISM IN SCHOOL by Barbara Harrison.
Actual account of what parents and teachers did to
effect change in a New York private school.

According to Piaget, that which adults call play is the "activity of intelligence" for children. And others have referred to play as the "work" of children.

By playing, children explore their environment, learn to be creative, and have confirmed for them what they "know" about the world.

Children make choices when playing and in doing so are active, rather than passive.

BUT.... what choices do they make? Does a child's sex influence her or his play choices? If so, how? why?

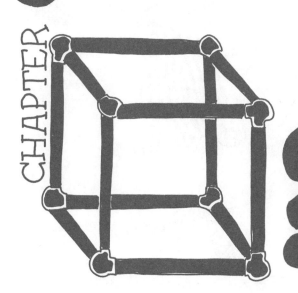

The purpose of this chapter is to explore the functions of play in the development of children's bodies, socio-emotional growth, and relationships with others, all as affected by their sex.

PLAY SKILLS

- types of play
- fallacies and facts on sex differences in children's play and body development
- awareness activities
- adult/child play activities
- resources

CLEANS/DIRTIES

WORK/PLAY CLOTHES

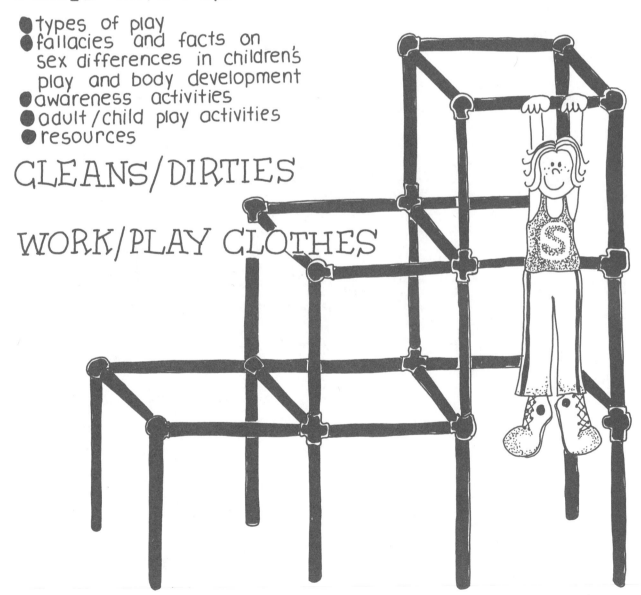

types of play

First, let's look at different types of play. According to Sutton-Smith (1971) there are four types of play associated with four forms of learning.

1. IMITATION Children copy others' acts and by doing so learn about and understand their world. Imitation becomes more generalized, i.e., copying adults in general during preschool years whereas in toddlerhood it's more specific--copying mommy. Sex-role imitation becomes increasingly prevalent during preschool years.

2. EXPLORATION Exploratory play involves children's analyzing the hows and whys of the workings of things and by doing so, learning to understand the connection between these things, places and people besides themselves. They begin to understand cause-and-effect relationships.

3. PREDICTION Predictive play involves children's starting to make predictions about and test out how they can have an effect on their world. The second year of life involves large motor testing... running, pulling, pushing. This form of play is "self validation".... "I can do it, and I can do it any way I want." In the preschool years GAMES become an important way children validate themselves by using others as their standard of competence. Competitiveness becomes integral to play as in the games "hide and seek" and "simon says".

4. CONSTRUCTION Very related to imitative and exploratory play... constructive play involves children's both figuratively and literally "putting things together" and by doing so, understanding their world. Dolls, toys, or imaginary companions may be used to define relationships in the world.

ask yourself

 Do all children get adequate exposure and encouragement to participate in these four types of play?

 Are all children, regardless of their sex, exposed to the SAME KINDS of experiences within each of these four types of play?

 What experiences is your child having with regards to these four types of play?

 Would your child be having different kinds of experiences if she/he were of the other sex?

Posters (Women's Movement, Children's Literature Cooperative, LTD)

"Busy Children".........pictures a boy knitting and a girl playing with a truck.

"Playground"...........shows young children playing together.

books

<u>MAKING FRIENDS</u>   by Eleanor Schick

Pictures a small boy on his way to the playground where he meets his friend, a young girl.

<u>GIRLS AND BOYS, BOYS AND GIRLS</u> by Eve Merriam

Multi-ethnic group of children play together unrestricted by sex-role stereotyping.

<u>HOW MANY KIDS ARE HIDING ON MY BLOCK?</u> by Jean Shulman

Multi-ethnic group of children play together on a city street.

Tee Hee......KNOCK KNOCK: Who's there?
CANOE
Canoe-who?
Canoe come out and play?

SEX ROLES AND PLAY

Preschoolers are usually fortunate in that they play with **whoever lives close by**, a child of her or his parents' friends or children at a preschool.

BUT The older preschool or elementary-age child is very likely to play predominantly with children of his/her same sex. AND, the older children become, the more sex-segregated their play groups are.

SOME RESEARCH FINDINGS

- Boys usually play in more competitive team games with more elaborate rules.
- Girls are more likely to play simple games with few rules, e.g., hopscotch.
- Girls are more likely to play "house" and play in activities that are related to domesticity and/or nurturing.

Children's play activities can make a difference in what they do as adults!

According to Booth (1972) boys (starting in late preschool years) learn group procedures and practices as well as initiative and competition through their participating in team activities, to which girls are not frequently exposed.

We wonder about this limitation imposed on girls and the effect it will have on them later on as adults when attempting to compete with males in careers.

BUT WHAT ABOUT CHILDREN?

The fact is that throughout childhood girls and boys are about the same in physical size and strength. If anything, girls are larger and stronger than boys during their **pre**adolescent years, 9-12, as they do reach adolescence earlier. Girls are roughly one year ahead in development when they enter elementary school. Yet, how many people continually think and say that little girls aren't capable of playing actively?

One major concern with having girls participate as fully as boys in sports and body development is that by doing so their appearance will be masculinized. And after all, who would find a muscular female attractive! THIS IS A FALLACY!

According to Dr. Harmon Brown, an endocrinologist and women's track coach, people's basic physiques are genetically determined. Athletic females are not going to develop massive bulging muscles....only if predisposed that way.

Will encouragement of young girls' developing body skills lead to health problems when they are adults? Rarick (1972) reports on research conducted on the effects of competitive sports on girls' growth, development and health.

MISCONCEPTIONS

GROWTH AND DEVELOPMENT......no growth impairment with swimmers; some accelerated growth.

SPORTS DURING MENSTRUAL PERIOD..... some disorders with overtraining; physical performance not affected.

CHILD-BEARING FUNCTIONS.....no adverse effects; athletes have fewer complications and shorter labor

MASCULINIZATION...... no evidence to support

PHYSIOLOGICAL FUNCTIONS.....more resistant than males to development of muscular strength and power; heart and respiratory adaptations to heavy training similar to males.

PSYCHOLOGICAL AND EMOTIONAL EFFECTS.....no evidence to support women unsuited for competitive sports.

A STEREOTYPE THAT MANY BELIEVE ooo boys are more able to, and should, engage in more physical, active and aggressive play than girls.

WHY? Most beliefs about children's abilities stem from beliefs about adults' abilities, which may not be appropriately compared. On the average, men are larger, stronger, and heavier than women. BUT, IT IS A FACT that these differences e.g. strength, are _far_ _greater_ _within_ _each_ _sex_ than the differences found between the sexes.

ACTIVITY LEVEL

Research indicates that activity level does not appear to be dependent on sex, as many people mistakenly believe. Activity level varies daily and yearly for each individual. when there are differences, they usually (but not always!) favor boys.
(Maccoby and Jacklin, 1974)

STRENGTH

Evidence shows that the difference in strength between males and females is dependent on athletic training... difference in strength is far less between _trained_ male and female athletes than it is between untrained males and females. The more training that females undergo, the stronger they get!

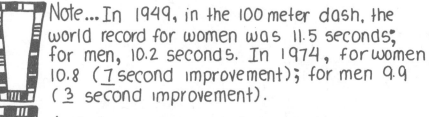

Note... In 1949, in the 100 meter dash, the world record for women was 11.5 seconds; for men, 10.2 seconds. In 1974, for women 10.8 (7 second improvement); for men 9.9 (3 second improvement).

And, in swimming, in the 1924 Olympics, in the 400 meter freestyle, the winning time for men was 16% faster than the women's; in 1972, only 7.3% faster. (Scott, 1974)

What will the differences be as more women become involved in sports?

SO, LET YOUR LITTLE GIRL BE A TOMBOY!

- 78% of 36 female college students reported having been tomboys as children.

- 60% of 34 junior high school age girls reported having been tomboys and 63% said they were tomboys AT PRESENT. The girls who reported themselves as being tomboys tended to have more educated mothers as well as preferring boys' games. (Hyde and Rosenberg, 1974)

- And, Helson (1965) found a consistent correlation between creativity in college women and their having been tomboys.

Thus, we believe it is very important to encourage both girls and boys to participate in activities in which they will be active, exert their energies and bodies, and, by doing so, develop body and play skills that will help them become active and physically coordinated adults... who are confident and proud of their bodies!

DO FOR/WITH CHILDREN!

WHAT YOU CAN

- Encourage preschool boys and girls to participate in the SAME body and play activities TOGETHER.

- Expose them to physically active, strong, alert and aggressive male and female role models.

- Arrange opportunities for safe contact activities.

- Provide them with the appropriate clothing for work and play.

AWARENESS ACTIVITIES

1 Examine your own beliefs and attitudes about sports. Should certain sports be limited to males? To females? Why? How could you argue the other point of view?

2 Observe preschoolers at a park or childcare center. Are ALL the boys engaged in sports activities and/or rough aggressive play? Are all the girls engaged in passive, non-competitive play? Are there any children engaged in non-traditional play?

3 List the favorite play activities of your child. After each, write what you think your child is learning or gaining from that activity, such as developing self-esteem, small-muscle coordination, etc.

ACTIVITY   GAIN

- throwing balls......large-muscle development, active play, predictive play
- playing with dolls...role playing (being a parent), imitation, constructive play
- _____   _____
- _____   _____
- _____   _____

Are there any skills your child has missed?

Ask a parent of a child of the other sex to do the same and compare the two lists.

4 Encourage your child to participate in play activities traditionally reserved for children of the other sex. Remember..... our goal is to help develop well rounded children (and consequently, adults), NOT to reverse traditional sex roles for people.

5 Watch women's basketball, wrestling, volleyball, gymnastics, etc., as well as men's.

PLAY AND BODY SKILL ACTIVITIES

Activities to encourage development of a variety of body and play skills include:

- rolling on the grass
- racing to the play structures
- watching and following a T.V. exercise program; helping each other do the exercises
- wrestling on an old mattress
- toe, finger, leg or arm wrestling
- walking on a balance beam
- hugging
- punching a clown stand-up punching bag
- PARENT-CHILD PARTICIPATION: ....running and playing tag, playing "statues," giving piggy back rides, actively participating at the playground, etc.
- setting up an obstacle course with tires, cardboard boxes, an old hose, etc.
- encouraging body contact skills for boys/girls
- welcoming preschoolers jumping to you, hanging on, crawling over, wiggling under, bear-hugging, etc.
- swimming, diving..... how about leap frog?
- Simon Says... run, hop, jump, crawl, etc.
- throwing or rolling balls for distance.
- gymnastic and ballet classes for boys and girls
- balloon volleyball (tie a piece of string across the room)
- other

By developing play and body skills, young children can also be developing their VOCABULARY. Talk with your child about ACTION WORDS that are associated with playing.....

- run   - dance
- kick   - throw
- hop   - hit
- push   - skip

YOGA for children, too! Children, as well as adults, can get in touch with individual parts of their bodies and develop skills of balance, control, agility and strength.

Be a Bird, Be a Frog, Be a Tree by Richard Carr
Yoga exercises for children
(Record also available)

77

the cleans & dirties

It is often outdoors that one sees the clearest division along sexist lines. Boys will be noisy, dirty, physical...... girls are not expected to get as dirty as boys. Girls are taught they must be careful about their clothes and appearance..... and they should be "ladies." Many children, especially girls, learn that cleanliness is a virtue..... that dirt is a "bad thing."

By heightening our own awareness of the materials that children naturally select for their play, we can develop patience, appreciation and understanding of a child's work.

Next time, before you voice loudly......... GET OUT OF THE MUD..... look at what these materials are providing for your preschooler.

- CONSTRUCTION with satisfaction
- DESTRUCTION without guilt
- OUTLET for aggression
- SENSE of mastery
- CHANCE for exploring forbidden interests
- OPPORTUNITY for fantasy experiences
- SENSORY pleasure and kinesthetic joy
- MEDIUM to experiment, construct, imitate, and explore..... that requires no special skills or achievement goals.

THE DIRTIES

Where can one find mud?
(DEFINITION of mud: soil+
sand+ water = mud)
Preschoolers have discovered
many interesting places:
● behind bushes
● near a leaky faucet
● in a puddle after the rain
● around a tree
● in the street beside the curb

One day you'll hear a squeal
of delight.... followed by
"LOOK, I mixed dirt and water
and I made mud."

In your yard, include one spot
for digging deep and making
mud. Your child (ren) won't need
it everyday, but it will be available when s/he or you need
it for relaxation, sensory
experimentation and manipulation.
Try it; you'll like it!

<u>MARGO MAKES A MESS</u> by Robert
and Tibby Stickgold (NSP)
Margo wants to make the biggest
mess in the world.

<u>RAIN RAIN RIVERS</u> by Uri Shulevitz
Little girls make creative messes
on rainy days.

<u>MARVELOUS MUD WASHING
MACHINE</u> by Patty Wolcott
A young boy experiences a
unique way to get clean.

<u>PETE'S PUDDLE</u> by Joanna Foster
and Beatrice Darwin
What to do with a puddle? Pete
in his big red boots... gives us
many ideas.

100 secret mud holes

HOW TO MAKE A PERFECT MUD HOLE
by Dirty Kidd

Put a hose in the soil, keeping
the hole full of water for
boats and wading. ● long
boards provide ramps for
toy cars ● big heavy rocks
can be pushed around as
stepping stones ● keep on
hand small shovels that really
dig ● add lots of water and
create "drip" castles ● add
a few dishes for creative
cookery. REMEMBER....
work clothes please!

GUSHY BOOK CO.

RESOURCE:
<u>MUD, SAND AND WATER</u>
  by Dorothy M. Hill
National Assoc. for the Educ. of
Young Children Activities Book

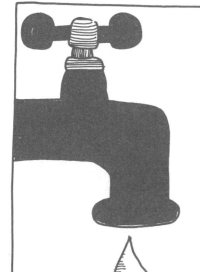

THE CLEANS

Hot day play activity or for clean-up....
After a messy fun time, use waterplay
to get your child clean. Put a little soap
in a large container (eg., plastic dishpan,
cooking pot, baby's bathtub, old ½ of a
tire).... add water toys, e.g., paper or
plastic cups, roast baster, funnel, straws,
empty frozen juice cans, squeeze bottles,
sponge, colander, corks, etc.

Washing the car, dishes or laundry;
watering the lawn; running through the
sprinkler.... are also different means of
hassle-free KID CLEANING.

Other waterplay activities include window
washing, giving his/her babydoll a bath,
watering outside plants, experimenting
with floating materials and water
painting the house.

RAINBOWS Look for a rainbow. Perfect
conditions are rain and sunshine. Sunlight
shines through the raindrops and scatters
into many colors--bands of colored light...
red, orange, yellow, green, blue......

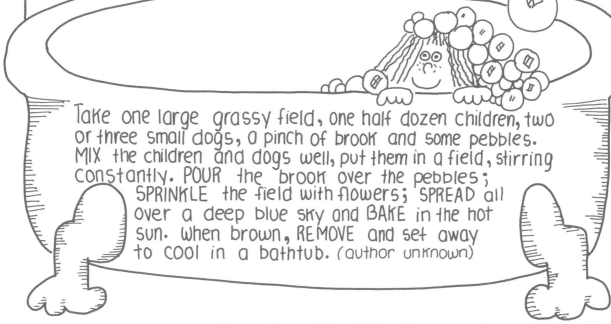

Take one large grassy field, one half dozen children, two
or three small dogs, a pinch of brook and some pebbles.
MIX the children and dogs well, put them in a field, stirring
constantly. POUR the brook over the pebbles;
SPRINKLE the field with flowers; SPREAD all
over a deep blue sky and BAKE in the hot
sun. When brown, REMOVE and set away
to cool in a bathtub. (author unknown)

work--play clothes

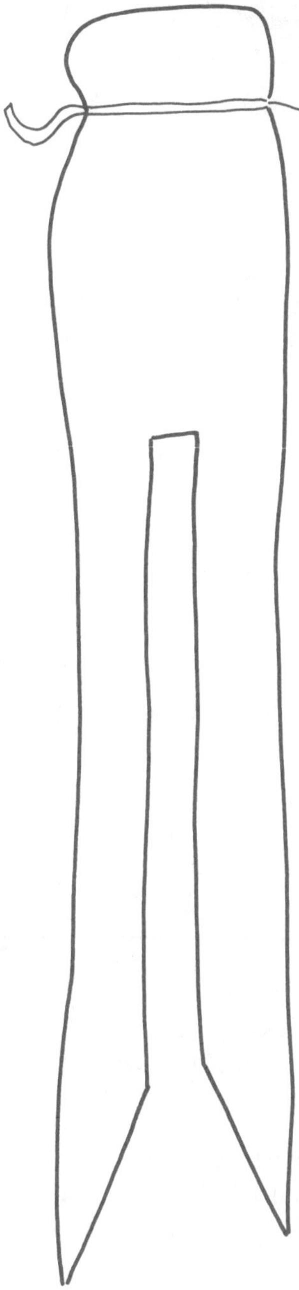

flexibility

protection

Play is a child's work. Children need to
be comfortable and free to work in
whatever they wear. Clothes are to
protect children's bodies from being hurt.
- crawling
- wrestling
- sliding
- tumbling
- rolling

all require protected bodies. AND,
appropriate clothing for the weather will
allow children to move more freely,
and be more relaxed!

stop

HIDDEN MESSAGES

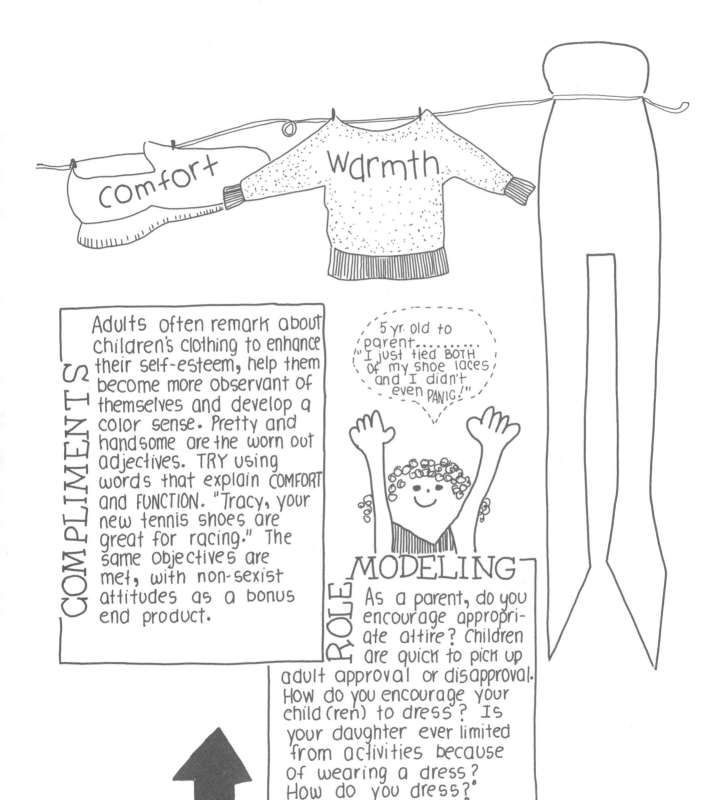

comfort

warmth

COMPLIMENTS

Adults often remark about children's clothing to enhance their self-esteem, help them become more observant of themselves and develop a color sense. Pretty and handsome are the worn out adjectives. TRY using words that explain COMFORT and FUNCTION. "Tracy, your new tennis shoes are great for racing." The same objectives are met, with non-sexist attitudes as a bonus end product.

5 yr. old to parent.....
"I just tied BOTH of my shoe laces and I didn't even PANIC!"

ROLE MODELING

As a parent, do you encourage appropriate attire? Children are quick to pick up adult approval or disapproval. How do you encourage your child(ren) to dress? Is your daughter ever limited from activities because of wearing a dress? How do you dress? THINK... comfort, warmth, protection and flexibility!

DON'T COLOR CODE YOUR KIDS!
Pastels, brights, darks, pink and blue for ALL!

PAPER PEOPLE

There will be days when your child will insist on trying on every stitch of clothing s/he owns. (Some days you are not quite ready to deal with this.)

1. Perfect time to create a paper person. Use large sheets of butcher paper. from the local market. Usually butchers are pleased to contribute.

2. Have your child lie down and trace his/her body. Siblings are often enthusiastic tracers.

3. Provide the supplies for your preschooler to dress her/his self with crayons, felt pens, poster paint, construction paper, etc.

4. Cut out the "dressed" body shape. This may require your assistance.

5. PLAY MAKEBELIEVE A look-a-like paper person can wear anything; go anywhere; and be anyone!

84

"C.A.P.T.....
children Are
People, TOO."
..... and others.
Send for
catalogue.....
White River Co.
25 Broadway
Elm-
wood
Park,
NJ
07407

RESOURCES

PUZZLE: "Dressing and Undressing"
A boy and girl of the same size are
holding fishing nets and fish. Their
clothing comes off, illustrating that
the only real difference between boys
and girls is a biological one (CC)

READ...... SUGAR PINK ROSE (WRPC)
by Adela Turin and Nella Bosnia

6. Paper people can be
used to learn the names
for different body parts
... elbow, neck, chin, big
toe, etc.

7. Make life-size paper dolls
from two identical body-shape
cut outs. Staple together and
stuff with crumpled newspaper.
Be sure to draw facial features
and other body designs before
stuffing. MY-SIZE paper dolls can
8. be used for dramatic play and
dressed with real clothes.

Project a photo slide of your
child in an active pose on to
a wall or movie screen. Tape on
large piece of butcher paper.
Have child trace outline and
then color with paint or pens.

I'd love to hear
TOMMY AND SARAH
DRESS UP by Guntilla Wolde
It's about a boy&girl try-
ing on all kinds of clothes

PLAYSKILL RESOURCES

toys and play apparatus

PLAY SCENES LOTTO (MB)
A full color, multi-cultural photographic lotto game which uses pictures of girls and boys in active play, free of sex stereotyped roles

BODY IMAGE PUZZLE (LM)
White boy, Black girl, Oriental boy

KIDS PUZZLE (CC)
Brightly-colored figures of children in motion

JOLLY SWING (CC)
Tubular snap-together pieces for climbing and swinging

PLAYDOME (CC)
Climbing apparatus

JOLLY GYM (CC)
Indoor/outdoor gym made of plastic tubes (Try making one yourself with plumbers' p.v.c.)

PUNCHING BAG ON STAND (CC)

JUMP-O-LEEN (CC)
An inflatable bouncing exerciser

PLAY-ALL (CC)
Three curved sectional polyethylene form seesaw, circle, recliner

books

SUGAR PINK ROSE by Adela Turin and Nella Bosnia (WRPC)
Gray male elephants and female elephants who are compulsorily pink learn that one shouldn't be limited by color or by what one wears.

LET'S PLAY by Gyo Fuji Kawa
Very active girls and boys play together. Good ethnic representation.

SHIMMY, SHIMMY, COKE-LA-POP! by Carol and John Langstaff
Photographs of girls in motion help illustrate games and rhymes. Good ethnic representation.

MUMBLES AND SNITS by Beverley Allinson
Mift, a female Mumble, and Stumble, a male snit, two fantasy-like creatures, teach other mumbles and snits that playing, dancing and singing can be fun anytime.

86

THE FEELIES

Humans are emotional,
as well as rational, beings. We
are able to FEEL as well as
THINK. We can react spontane-
ously at a "gut level" based on
how we feel about something,
or we can hold in our feelings
and let our thought processes
take over to determine
the "appropriate" way
to act.

CHAPTER 4

Children usually act more
on a feeling level, while
adults act more on a
thinking, or cognitive
level.

Expressing one's feelings is important. It can help in communicating honestly and openly with others; getting in touch with our own reactions to stimuli; and, as an emotional release, in alleviating nerves, anxiety, anger, etc.

Too often males do not express their feelings. They have learned it is "feminine" or "sissyish" to cry or show fear. Instead, they should be "cool, calm, collected." But, it is believed by many that this type of orientation is a significant contribution to the development of ulcers, heart disease, neuroses, etc.

And, too often females do not express ANGER. Many believe it would be unfeminine to do so. But by not doing so, many females have not learned to be assertive and to stand up for themselves and/or for what they believe.

The purpose of this chapter is to provide activities and resources to use in encouraging children to express ALL their emotions and to understand that to do so is positive, healthy and okay.

YOU WILL FIND

- information on the relationship between feelings and sex roles
- general activities to facilitate the learning about and expressing of feelings
- activities and resources pertaining to specific feelings

WHAT ARE THE FEELIES

Think of the wide range of feelings you experience (whether or not you actually express them)......... anger, fear, sadness, worry, aggression, caring, jealousy, envy, enthusiasm, tenderness, nervousness, surprise, helplessness, rage, depression, gloom, resentment, joy, annoyance, defiance, hostility, insecurity, and others.

NOW, CHECK THOSE WHICH YOU EXPRESS RATHER THAN KEEP INSIDE.

? Would you react differently to a <u>child's</u> expressing these emotions based on the child's sex? For example, do you ever think or say, "Big boys don't cry" or "Little ladies don't shout"?

? Would you have checked the same if you were of the other sex?

Now, let's look at some activities which can help your preschooler learn about the "feelies" and how to express them. You can devise others by extrapolating from what we have presented here.

The first step in dealing with feelings is getting them OUT! Feelings can be..........

TALKED ABOUT
ACTED OUT
INVENTORIED

TALKING

TALK TIME will encourage learning to communicate, open up and share, adult to child and child to adult. During a quiet, snuggly and comfortable space.............share:

What is one thing I DO/YOU DO that makes you (<u>sad,</u> happy, scared, etc.)?

SONGS.....Sometimes young children need a more indirect vehicle for acting out their feelings. Sing the following song together, pantomining the words. Make up your own verses, too.

If you're happy and you know it, clap your hands....(repeat), If you're happy and you know it, then your face will surely show it....If you're happy and you know it, clap your hands.
- angry....stomp your feet
- sad.....wipe a tear
- jealous....make a face
- scared....shake like this
- other.......................

GAME How Would You Feel? (HWYF?) Create a situation fashioned for a certain emotional response. Ask HWYF? Talk about the situation and the alternatives. FEELING SITUATIONS:
- A bully takes away your tricycle. HWYF?
- Big sister brings home a baby mouse for you. HWYF?
- You found your missing tennis shoe. HWYF?
- Your brother turns the channel on the TV when you're watching a program. HWYF?
- You are having artichokes for breakfast. HWYF?

RECORDS
Hap Palmer
(Educational Activities, Inc.)
"Feelin' Free"
"Getting to Know Myself"

Mr. Rogers' Record Album
(Pickwick Label)
"You Are Special"

ACTING

FEELINGS TIME

When your child is feeling something very intensely, ask her/him HOW s/he is feeling—what does s/he feel like doing? Encourage him/her to EXPRESS the feeling by
- shouting
- shaking all over
- running
- crying
- laughing
- other ....

Allow her/him to act out the feeling that s/he may have thought to be "unacceptable" without fear of being judged.

As the child matures, talk about how feelings can be expressed in different situations without offending others.

MAKING FACES

A person has 16 different muscles in her/his face that can work together to make "oodles" of expressions..... just think of the possibilities!

Keep available a hand and/or a large child level wall mirror. Children need to be able to see the facial expressions their feelings are projecting.

READ the book FRANCES FACE-MAKER by William Cole. When Francis doesn't want to go to bed, her parent uses a face-making game to entice her to bed. Reread the story (keep a mirror on hand):
- pantomime the story
- role play the face-making game
- take turns making the faces.

WRITE your own face-making story, e.g.,"Face Making While Food Tasting" (salt, chocolate, lemons, sugar, pickles, etc.).

"Photo Face-Making"-Look at pictures in magazines. Imitate the feeling faces you find.

GAME: How do people look when they are: hungry, mad, scared ? Child answers with a face, adult imitates.

CHARADES

Write a variety of emotional response situations on slips of paper (or, for preschoolers, whisper in her/his ear). For example:

- frustration — trying to tie shoe laces
- fear — lost in a big department store
- joy — jumping in puddles
- surprise — a frog jumped into your lunch box
- anger — cleaning up your room all by yourself after your friends leave.

Act out the situation. Your audience guesses the "feeling" situation. and the emotional response. How about after the dinner dishes are done, end your evening in charades.

Other ideas:

- _____
- _____
- _____
- _____
- _____

PUPPETS

Puppets are good for practicing problem solving. Present a question. "How do you feel when someone hits you?" Try it. You can be the "hitter" to start the action going. Act out the scene. Talk about the alternatives to solving the problem..... then try them.

This is basically a role-playing technique except that you're using puppets instead of putting a person "on the spot."

Be sure to get your audience involved!

PROPS

Props are important for exploring emotions. The play house and play people are valuable to children for acting out conflicts and feelings about home and family members. You can use them more directly by creating a story. Start acting out the story and when you reach a critical point give the dolls or play people to the child and let her/him finish the story.
Examples of books*:

WILL I HAVE A FRIEND?

IRA SLEEPS OVER

THE DEAD BIRD

WHAT MARY JO SHARED

* see feelies books—pp. 100-101.

JOY pain fear SURPRISE

INVENTORYING

STEP OUTSIDE YOURSELF Take some time to inventory your "feeling style" ......the way you approach children emotionally. NOTICE
- the tone of your voice
- body contact with a child
- physical space (how close or distant you are to a feeling situation)
- body language
- pattern for resolving a problem.

Love anger

WOULD YOU REACT THE SAME TO A:
- boy.... girl
- adult
- group of preschoolers
- older child
- your child
- a friend's child ?

FEELING BOOK

Assemble a snapshot book of your child's feelings. Use construction paper stapled together or a commercial scrapbook, with one photo per page and space for describing the picture and emotional responses. Include pictures of your child expressing love, anger, pain, surprise, jealousy, aggression, etc. Examples:
- holding your new baby
- a surprise birthday party
- being sick or hurt
- hugging
- having fun with a friend
- sharing a lunch.

OR cut out magazine pictures of other people expressing feelings.

Show your "customed" photo book to the main character... your preschooler. Talk about the situation, the feeling, and the reaction to the feeling. Then, write about it under the photo.

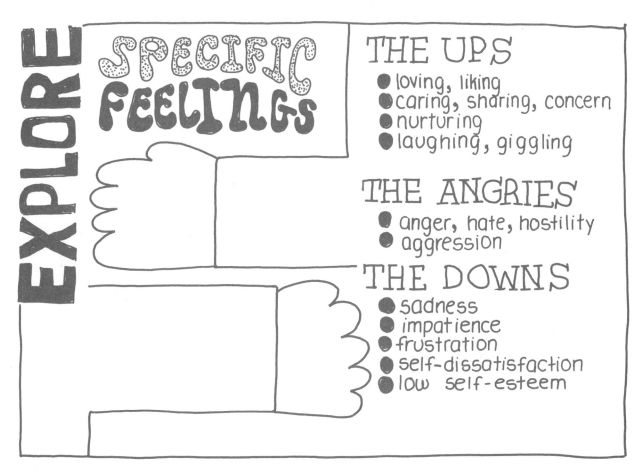

EXPLORE

SPECIFIC FEELINGS

THE UPS
- loving, liking
- caring, sharing, concern
- nurturing
- laughing, giggling

THE ANGRIES
- anger, hate, hostility
- aggression

THE DOWNS
- sadness
- impatience
- frustration
- self-dissatisfaction
- low self-esteem

FEELINGS ARE OUR FRIENDS

PAT PALMER

It's a great day and I'm a great person.
CUT OUT AND WEAR.

FEEL DEEPLY ENJOY SIMPLY THINK FREELY
BE WHO YOU REALLY ARE!

MOOD INDICATOR
I AM FEELING
- cool
- right on
- great
- super
- ya'hoo
- fantastic

- lousy
- ugh
- moan
- blah
- picky picky
- gloom

THE UPS

STRAIGHT FACE

NO TICKLING ALLOWED...... try to make your child laugh in 2 min. while s/he attempts to keep a straight face. Take turns. NO TOUCHING.

INITIATE A "WHISPER DAY" OR AT LEAST A "WHISPER HOUR." THIS IS YOUR MENTAL HEALTH BREAK!

Whisper day

POSSIBLY AN "INCENTIVE" WILL BE NECESSARY TO INSURE A SUCCESSFUL M. H. B. ..... BUT IT WOULD BE WELL WORTH IT!

CARING

Talk about what caring means. Definition: being concerned; being attentive to people's needs.

Talk about places that care for people.... school, hospitals, the home, etc.

Take on a new "caring" situation with your child:
- a new pet
- arrange to babysit a neighbor's baby.
- visit patients at a nursing home

Construct a caring mobile. Find in magazines, draw, etc:
- 5 things your child takes care of (dog, fish, toys, etc.)
- 5 things s/he cares about (comfort blanket, big bed etc.)
- 5 people who care about her/him. ASSEMBLE........ ..... tie pictures on a coat hanger with yarn. This activity can provide practice in cutting, tying, glueing, and stapling skills.

BELLY • BUTTON • BOUNCE

When several children are around, play BBB. Everyone lying on the floor-resting her/ his head on a bellybutton. Each person receives a number, 1, 2, 3, etc. On the signal "bounce," each person calls out his/her number in order. GOAL: call out all the numbers without laughing.

TOE WRESTLING

Two children sit on the floor facing each other with both arms wrapped around their own knees and toes touching each other's toes. GOAL: to get his/her toes under the other child's toes and roll them over backwards. Best played barefooted! For variety... apply massive amounts of mud, butter, catsup, pudding, lotion or any combination of these materials.

THE ANGRIES

CRANKIE CLASHING

LET'S HAVE A: SCRAMBLE, FIGHT, SKIRMISH, CLASH, CONFLICT!
FOR WHEN WE'RE: ANGRY, FRUSTRATED, MAD, STUCK WITH "EXTRA" ENERGY!

Today it's O.K.! We all need a mad time occassionally. Have your preschooler crush newspaper into balls. Arrange cardboard boxes for "hide-behind" and protection. Use several boxes in different areas of the yard to encourage alternative places to hide and throw.

Get preschooler to load up with newspaper balls and take cover behind a box..... LET IT GO!! GET IT ALL OUT!! GET INVOLVED!! Your child will enjoy playing with you, too.

If you engage in a house version of crankie-clashing, try chunks of styrofoam or sponge for throwing.... less noisy and harmful. Try marshmallows if you're hungry! VALUE: NO ONE GETS HURT AND FEELINGS ARE PLAYED OR WORKED OUT.

Materials: egg cartons for smashing, boxes for kicking, pillows for punching, paper for ripping, batakas for zapping.

AGGRESSION COOKIES: BEAT: ¾ CUP MARGARINE, 1 CUP BROWN SUGAR, 1 EGG, ¾ CUP WATER, 1 TSP VANILLA...... ADD: ½ TSP SODA, ½ TSP SALT, 2 CUPS OATS, 1 CUP FLOUR.

GIVE.....each child one portion to beat, roll, squeeze, smash and smack.

BAKE.....preheat oven to 350. Bake 12-15 min. For variety, add carob chips, nuts, coconut, etc.

Preschoolers can pretend the cookie dough is somebody s/he is mad at. Encourage child to verbalize feelings. When all the "aggression" is out, drop by teaspoon on cookie sheet, mash flat, sprinkle with sugar.

When a person needs a "warm fuzzie," a "stroke" or to hear all those good things about her/himself ...a boost to her/his self-esteem, it's time to create a "fuzzie" or PMA......... (positive mental attitude) mobile.

A warm fuzzie

Everyone occasionally "gets down!"

In the shape of the human body, cut 12" geometric shapes (head and body = circles, arms and legs = rectangles, feet and hands = triangles); use cardboard or construction paper. Fasten the body parts together with paper brads. Add facial features and yarn for hair.

Select someone for this week's fuzzie personality. Have each family member write all the things s/he likes about the person. Be specific and personal. For example: Sandy made me laugh today; Sandy can count to ten; Sandy gives neat bear hugs, etc.

When situations arise, add them to the mobile...right then; immediate positive reinforcement. Also, glue, staple, tape or write and add... a photo or two, a surprise, a physical description, likes and dislikes, favorite this or that.

When the MOMENT arrives that a "positive stroke" is needed, read the mobile to the child or adult. WARM FUZZIES are especially appreciated during times of stress. Consider this activity prior to the holidays, school exams, hospital stays, arrival of a new baby, moving, etc. You will be ready with a positive alternative.

NO-FUSS BUSY BAG

Sometimes feelings need to be alleviated for adults as well as for children. TRY THE NO-FUSS BUSY BAG...... a sanity saver for "BIG" people. The next time your preschooler is bored, impatient or frustrated... which can cause lots of feelings to come out of YOU... use the NO-FUSS BAG.

WHEN TO USE IT Almost any outing where <u>waiting</u> is involved. It will save adults from countless extra conflicts and mini-frustrations. Somehow the expression "busy hands are happy hands" pops into mind.

WHAT TO USE: child's back pack, old hand bag or purse, large brown paper bag, or plastic bag with handle.

WHAT TO INCLUDE: Three...... "surprise" items as well as a snack item; throw in a wash cloth just in case.

- scissors, paper, tape
- deck of cards
- finger puppets
- sticker and/or small picture books
- finger foods
- old toy that's been forgotten
- pipe cleaners
- felt pens, paper.

WHAT NOT TO INCLUDE: noisy items, messy foods, and surprises with too many small pieces or intricate parts.

"FEELIE" BOOKS

FEELING BOOKS CAN BE USED TO:
- explore feelings we all have
- set the action for dramatic play
- pantomime
- give puppet shows
- explore alternative solutions and/or approaches to feelings

FEELINGS Inside You and Out Loud Too
  by Barbara Kay Polland
Explores the feelings of: frustration, private, special, fear, love, pain, good, jealous, close and alone. Presents ways to think about, talk about and understand emotions. Excellent photographs of young children.

A book which we highly recommend and which includes activities for "talking about," acting out, and inventorying feelings: LIKING MYSELF   by Pat Palmer (IP) In this activities book we find that feelings are "good friends" and are important in telling us things about ourselves. It's okay to have ALL kinds of feelings, even ones like anger and grief. People can accept us even when we express these kinds of feelings. Special attention is paid to the belief that it's okay for men and boys to cry, feel hurt, scared and lonesome.

BOOKS DEALING WITH SPECIFIC FEELINGS

- caring
- sharing
- loving

I LOVE GRAM   by Ruth Sonneborn
BEST FRIENDS   by Myra Berry Brown
THE BOY WITH A PROBLEM by Joan Fassler
THE STORY OF FERDINAND by Munro Leaf
BIG SISTER AND LITTLE SISTER by Charlotte Zolotow
I LOVE MY MOTHER   by P. Zindel
WE'RE VERY GOOD FRIENDS, MY BROTHER AND I
    by Patrick Hallinan

● hurt
● pain
● sadness
● loneliness

● anger
● hate
● mad
● jealousy

FEEL

● shyness
● uncertainty

● fear

● general feelings

GROWNUPS CRY, TOO by Nancy Hazen (LP)
THE DEAD BIRD by Margaret Wise Brown
ABOUT DYING by Sara Bonnett Stern
THE TENTH GOOD THING ABOUT BARNEY by Judith Viorst
FOREVER LAUGHTER by Don Freeman
THE LAST VISIT by Doug Jamieson (BWS)
TELL ME, MR. ROGERS by Fred Rogers

PLEASE MICHAEL, THAT'S MY DADDY'S CHAIR
   by Susan Elizabeth Mark (BWS)
WE ARE HAVING A BABY by Vicki Holland
BETSY'S BABY BROTHER by Gunilla Wolde
PETER'S CHAIR by Erza Jack Keats
IF IT WEREN'T FOR YOU by Charlotte Zolotow
ON MOTHER'S LAP by Ann Herbert Scott
NOBODY ASKED ME IF I WANTED A BABY SISTER
   by Martha Alexander

THAT MAKES ME MAD! by Steven Kroll (BBP)
THE TEMPER TANTRUM BOOK by Edna Mitchell Preston
RUNAWAY JOHN by Leonore Klein
BOY, WAS I MAD by Kathryn Hitte
THE HATING BOOK by Charlotte Zolotow
THINGS I HATE by Harriet Wittles and Joan Greisman
I DO NOT LIKE IT WHEN MY FRIEND COMES TO VISIT
   by Ivan Sherman
MINOO'S FAMILY by Sue Crawford (BWS)

I AM ADOPTED by Susan Lapsley
DIVORCE IS A GROWN UP PROBLEM: A BOOK ABOUT
DIVORCE FOR YOUNG CHILDREN AND THEIR PARENTS
   by Janet Senberg
WILL I HAVE A FRIEND by Miriam Cohen
IRA SLEEPS OVER by Bernard Waber
FREE AS A FROG by Elizabeth Jamison Hodges

THERE'S A NIGHTMARE IN MY CLOSET by Mercer Mayer
WHAT'S THAT NOISE? by Lois Kauffman
WHAT MARY JO SHARED by Janice May Udry
MICHAEL IS BRAVE by Helen E. Buckley

I HAVE FEELINGS by Terry Berger
T.A. FOR TOTS AND OTHER PRINZES by Alvyn M. Freed
HAPPY, SAD, SILLY, MAD by Barbara Shook Hazen

5 LIVING SKILLS

LIVING SKILLS

CHILD CARE

the Kid

YARDWORK

HOUSEKEEPING

CHAPTER **5**

HEALTH CARE

HOME GARDEN

HEALTH CHILD CARE

MEAL PREPARATION

LOVE IS CLEANING UP YOUR OWN MESS

HOME MAINTENANCE

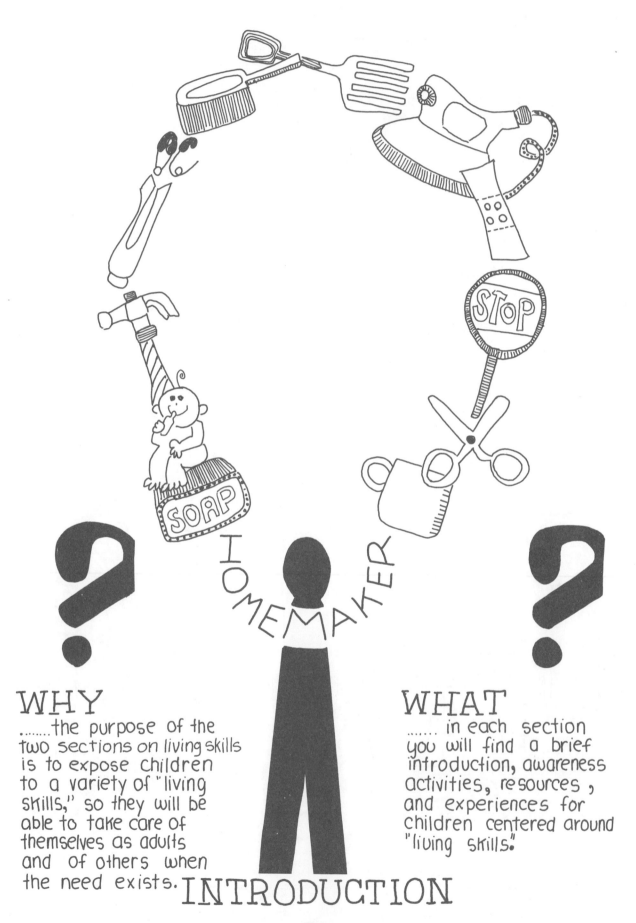

WHY

........the purpose of the two sections on living skills is to expose children to a variety of "living skills," so they will be able to take care of themselves as adults and of others when the need exists.

WHAT

...... in each section you will find a brief introduction, awareness activities, resources, and experiences for children centered around "living skills."

INTRODUCTION

As we all know, taking care of our own (and usually others') basic needs -- eating, bathing, having clean clothes -- is not always an easy task.

While traditionally, the breadwinning / gardening / home maintenance responsibilities have been reserved for males... AND the housekeeping/meal preparation/ nurturing responsibilities for females, this division of labor is not always functional. Consider the following situations....

- WHO takes care of the children and the house when the mother works more than the father?
- WHO does the necessary tasks when a man lives alone, or with other male roommates?
- WHO does the necessary cleaning / cooking / child rearing when both parents work?
- WHO does the yard and maintenance work in a household without a man?

The traditional system has been found to be counter-productive for many. YOUNG MALES: when they reach adulthood and don't know how to take care of their stomachs, their grooming, their homes -- without restaurants, maids, cooks or wives. YOUNG FEMALES: when they reach adulthood & don't know how to do light repairs or keep up the yard without a man. WHAT WE'RE SAYING IS that the reality of today's world is that males and females should and can learn all the daily "need" responsibilities -- what we call LIVING SKILLS -- as well as other skills for outside employment.

AWARENESS ACTIVITIES

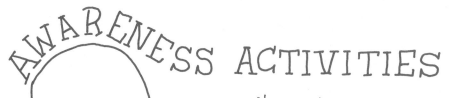

Now, let's first try out some things to see how children have been channeled into following a traditional division of labor.

SURVEY some of the following to see WHO handles living skill responsibilities........... male or female.

- Toy packaging of L.S.* toys at a toy store, eg., irons, hammers, tea sets, yard tools, etc.
- L.S. toy ads in department store catalog
- Television commercials advertising L.S. products
- Magazine advertising for L.S. products
- Television commercials advertising preschool L.S. toys

* L.S. = LIVING SKILL

HOW can these influence young children as to how they view the appropriateness of males and females in these roles?

LIVING SKILLS WORKER

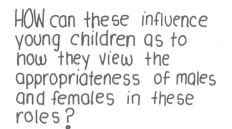

REQUIREMENTS ......intelligent, good health, energy, patience, sociability. SKILLS: at least 12 different occupations. HOURS: 99.6 per week. SALARY: none. HOLIDAYS: none. (will be required to remain on stand-by 24 hours a day, seven days a week). OPPORTUNITIES FOR ADVANCEMENT: none (limited transferability of skills acquired on the job). JOB SECURITY: none (trend is towards more layoffs, particularly as employee approaches middle age). FRINGE BENEFITS: food, clothing, and shelter generally provided, but additional bonuses will depend on financial standing and good nature of employer. No Social Security or pension plan (Anne Crittenden Scott, 1972).

108

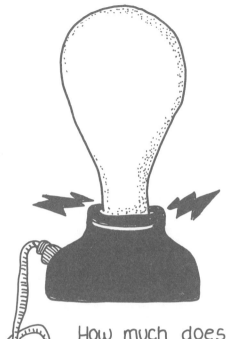

Are you curious as to what it would cost to employ a LIVING SKILLS WORKER to take care of you and your home? Social Security Research (Love, 1976) places the average American homemaker's economic value for all ages at $4,705 annually and for the peak years of 25-29, $6,417. Think how much it would cost today!

How much does each family member actually save by sharing the workload in your home? Use the LIVING SKILLS WORKER TIMECARD to figure each person's "weekly worth." The Department of Labor has current hourly rates for most skilled and semi-professional occupations. The following are a few to help you in your computations:

COOK..............$6.36+
chauffeur..........6.62+
dishwasher........5.29+
housekeeper......5.29+
bookkeeper.......3.38+
plumber...........7.42+
carpenter.........7.42+

L·S·WORKER TIME CARD

EMPLOYEE	HOURS	WAGE	OCCUPATION
Brother Matt			
	2½	$5.29	Dishwasher
	6	.75	Sitter
	1½	6.36	Cook

PLACE OF EMPLOYMENT __Smith Home__

SALARY $27.27

- Start activities in a positive, polite and personal manner. If you have the "crankies," wait for another time.

- Use a philosophy of "let's share," rather than one of "you do it," so that children understand that everybody— Dad, Mom, Sister, Brother, friends, guests.........who ever.... needs to chip in.

- Remember that it is the process, not the product, that is important. Show a child how to do a task.... provide the right tools.   Experiment and learn!

- Remember that all living skill activities are for both girls and boys.

- Preschoolers are great imitators. Role playing is a learning technique for their play/work world. SO.... slow down and take the time to do everything the correct and most logical way "from a child's point-of-view."

- Preschoolers want to be near their parents, teachers, etc., doing what they are doing. Although it will initially seem bothersome, welcome their efforts. Each time a task is repeated, watch the skill improve.

- Try not to use the word "work," especially in a negative tone. Often it can cut off spontaneous enthusiasm.

- Since preschoolers are infamous for their short attention span, break down a task into stages. Speak slowly and at their eye level. Be sure to check the completed task and compliment right away.... before the job is undone.

- Remember that mistakes can happen. Milk that is spilled the moment dinner is served is OK.

- Let children see, by what you do, the joy of accomplishment. Compliment yourself, OUTLOUD." Wow! I really worked hard planting this tree. Someday it will keep us cool on a hot day." Verbal modeling works wonders on building self-esteem.

- Lastly, and most importantly, it has been well documented in child development research that the behavior of adult models strongly influences children's ways of feeling, thinking and behaving. In other words, to be freed from sex role stereotypes BEFORE they are internalized and finalized, children need non-sexist adult role models.

- So, get started,... enjoy the newspaper delivered to the breakfast table, a non-sexist kitchen pet, some meal egg-speriments, a sure cure for hiccups and other "living skill" activities which you will find in these chapters.

- Margaret Mead's "Definition of a Home" will set these chapters in motion.

DEFINITION OF A HOME...

"Home Is a Place Where We Create the Future....

- the place where children are prepared to grow towards independence

- a way of living in the wider world

- and families set the launching process in motion."

HOME & GARDEN

HOUSEKEEPING

- dusting
- sweeping
- bed making
- picking up
- putting away
- the trash

- laundering
- ironing
- sewing

Preschoolers "enjoy" helping with housekeeping. Zero in on this time to teach living skills. Demonstrate that whether they are females or males they will need the "know-how" when they are adults.

Learning skills helps teach young children responsibilities...the responsibility of cleaning up after themselves... of participating in daily chores associated with running a household, etc.

THIS SECTION INCLUDES activities for people to get involved in the living skills associated with housekeeping.

HELPING

Agatha Fry, she made a pie,
And Christopher John helped bake it.
Christopher John he mowed the lawn,
And Agatha Fry helped rake it.

Zachary Zugg took out the rug,
And Jennifer Joy helped shake it,
And Jennifer Joy, she made a toy,
And Zachary Zugg helped break it.

And some kind of help
Is the kind of help
That helping's all about.
And some kind of help
Is the kind of help
We can all do without.
            by Shel Silverstein

Sometime when there is a small cluster of preschool children around... ASK them about housework. It could be an excellent time for CONSCIOUSNESS RAISING!

ASK?

- Whose role is housework?
- What does it entail?
- Is it only for men? women?
- If so, why?
- How do you feel about housework?
- Should boys do housework?
- What do mothers do for children?
- What do fathers do for children?

PICK UP...PUT AWAY

Put your things away,
Don't delay,
Let's help each other
Have a happy day!

Before the "pick up/put away" task becomes an ongoing source of conflict.... introduce it early in the preschool years in a game-like enjoyable form. The "pick-up/put away" habit will help preschoolers develop:
- organizational skills
- the value of taking care of one's possessions, and
- a happier YOU!

1. This needs to be a "togetherness task." Be consistent. Encourage children to put things back where they belong right after they are finished playing.

2. Arrange toys in groups to make cleaning up easier, eg., puzzles, books, games, etc.

3. Read TOMMY CLEANS HIS ROOM by Gunilla Wolde. Tommy plays a lot while looking for his bear.

4. This can be a time to practice following directions. "Let's put away everything by the chair....I'll put away the blocks... You put away the dolls... Get set.... Go!"

5. Select one special time each day to get things cleaned up and put away. Practice language skills, listen to a favorite record, make up songs, and play games... like "Simon Says."

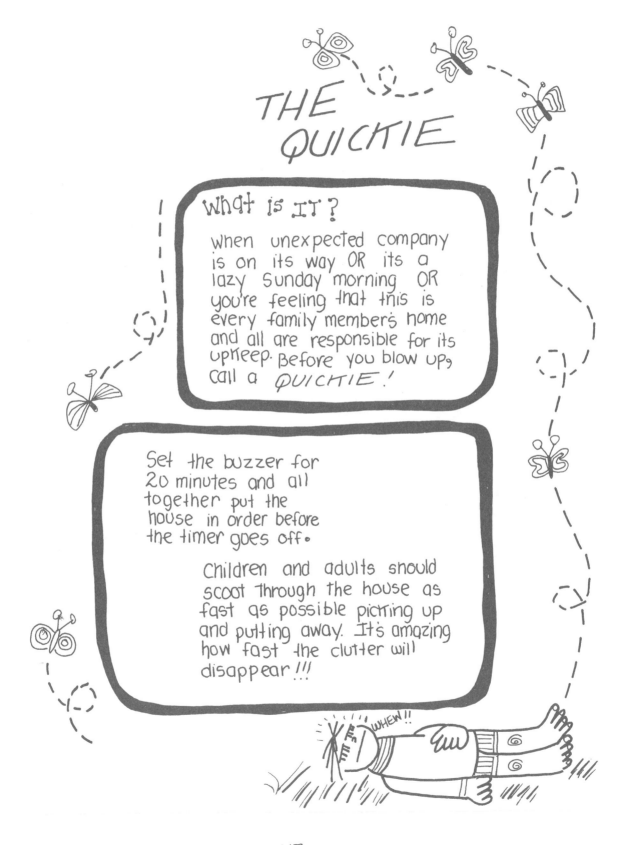

THE QUICKIE

What is IT?

When unexpected company is on its way OR its a lazy Sunday morning OR you're feeling that this is every family member's home and all are responsible for its upkeep. Before you blow up, call a *QUICKIE!*

Set the buzzer for 20 minutes and all together put the house in order before the timer goes off.

Children and adults should scoot through the house as fast as possible picking up and putting away. It's amazing how fast the clutter will disappear!!!

WHEW!!

DUSTING

As even a preschooler can notice.... by looking or by feeling, dust accumulates quickly. Dust can be unpleasant to look at as well as uncomfortable healthwise for persons with allergies.

SO, dusting is something that needs to be done and can be done easily by preschoolers. It is also an activity in which children can see immediate results.

Children can even make their own "dusters" with your help:
- a wash cloth with iron-on or felt facial features
- a large old soft glove
- an old woolen sock.

PLUS, dusting is an excellent time to practice new words. Together, you can dust UNDER the chair, ON TOP OF the table, IN the cupboard . . . .

THIS IS DUST

GROUND UP

black widow web

saw bug

wooley catipilar fur

cat whisker

bird feather

butterfly wing

eye lash

lady bug antenna

It's more than just bits of grit and dirt. Looked at through a microscope, dust is a mixture of all the above and much more.

START Fuzzies live everywhere; Dust, fur, fluff and hair; Find them, collect them, store them, share them; clean the house while you enjoy them!!!

Look for different types of fuzzies, e.g., rug, wall, clothes dryer (lint), pet fur, etc.

PET&FUZZIE

What am I? a friend to smother with T.L.C.*, a conversation piece, more colorful than a rubber band collection...

What to do!
● Draw a face on a clear glass jar (hint: use poster paint with a little white glue added, sharpie ink pens or enamel).
● Name your fuzzie.
● Watch it grow. Feed daily from dust clumps collected from behind doors, under beds, etc.
● Now you have a "pet," cleaner floors and a little laughter.

*T.L.C. ... Tender Loving Care

FLUFFY

DUSTY

"Pet fuzzies" sure are fun to play hide and seek with !!!

SWEEPING

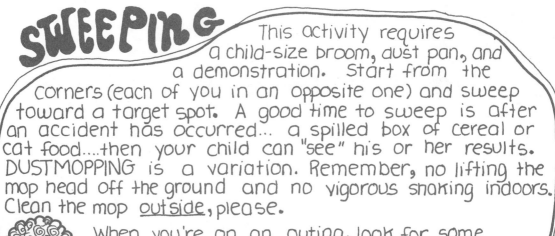

This activity requires a child-size broom, dust pan, and a demonstration. Start from the corners (each of you in an opposite one) and sweep toward a target spot. A good time to sweep is after an accident has occurred... a spilled box of cereal or cat food....then your child can "see" his or her results. DUSTMOPPING is a variation. Remember, no lifting the mop head off the ground and no vigorous shaking indoors. Clean the mop <u>outside</u>, please.

When you're on an outing, look for some examples of "sweepers"..... department-store sweepers, street sweepers, sidewalk sweepers. WHO DOES IT? WHAT DO THEY USE?

VACUUMING

The vacuum cleaner is such an awkward contraption! Some children are afraid of it and some are fascinated! A number one fear of preschoolers is that they could be sucked right in. To prevent this fear from developing, show your child(ren) that something big such as a pillow cannot get pulled in. BUT, at the same time, it is important that they understand that there are large power head vacuums inside that could HURT children if the vacuum is not used carefully and appropriately.

- Empty the bag and show that there is nothing but dust and fluff inside.
- Let your preschooler vacuum up a few small and familiar objects so that an understanding can develop of how things can be recovered.
- This activity can be turned into a simple game of VACUUM and IDENTIFY.
- Also, give yourself an "atta-person!" (pat on the back) for allowing this positive learning experience to happen.

? WHAT IS A BED

To a child a bed is:
- a secret hiding spot
- a home for her/his stuffed animals
- a trampoline
- a peaceful place to dream
- a possession to share with a friend
- place to be warm and be comforted
- and a "challenge to make!"

A few simple suggestions:
- To avoid the "wrinkles," use a quilt if possible.
- Use a fitted bottom sheet.
- Demonstrate how to pull the top sheet back to remove sand, socks and other goodies that become hidden under the covers AND then pull the sheet forward, followed by the blanket.... tuck in the sides together.
- Next the quilt and an eager "pillow fluffer" (Pillow fluffing is a great energy and anger release.)
- Older children can fold back the spread, lay the pillow on top and cover the pillow.
- If you teach this step-by-step pattern and a reason for each step..... there will be fewer frustrations and better bed making.

READ... THE BED BOOK by Sylvia Plath
A beautifully illustrated book of a poem about imaginative kinds of beds.

Trash, trash everywhere
Let all the people soon beware
Our "waste in haste" will
    cover our land
Unless we're clever,
Get the situation in hand.

A pop can here,
A plastic wrap there,
If we don't care enough,
We'll have a mountain of STUFF.

Miles and miles.....
Piles and piles,.....
Unsightly debris
Will cover the ground
Maybe EVEN you and me!

Let's all be wise
Let's all be clever,
We'll recycle our trash,
Have resources forever.

TRASH

Litterbugs away, litterbugs away,
Do not return! Stay away!

Trash in can,
    Garbage on the ground.
Recyclables will always be 'round.
Save your bottles, save your cans,
Today's efficiency is in your hands.
Clean beaches we'll have, neat cities, too.
We'll all live better,... both me and you!

STYRO-FOAM

by d.g.p.

First of all, preschoolers LIKE to take out the trash. Alternate this never-ending job between female and male, adults and children. There are many types of trash to collect.... bedroom, bathroom, garden, garage, local park, etc.

Taking out the trash can be a lesson in saving the land for children. Introduce the word "recycle". Set up three small containers for glass, metal and paper. Get your preschooler to collect and sort the recycle-ables.

Next time you come home from grocery shopping, let your child unwrap the groceries before putting them away. Put every piece of unnecessary wrapping in a wastebasket.

- TALK about the cellophane, styrofoam, egg cartons, paper bags, toothpaste boxes, etc.
- ASK your child if all these wrappings were really necessary.
- THINK and TALK about the clouds of soot that pollute the air when the trash is burned..... and all the chemicals from the plastics.

So that the TRASHOUT will hopefully soon FADEOUT, see if you and your preschooler(s) can cut back on the amount of trash that fills the trash cans each week.

Read LITTERBUGS COME IN EVERY SIZE by Norah Smaridge. It's a well illustrated cartoon version of the behavior of "neatos" and "litterbugs" and their effect on the environment.

Find visual aids (pictures, films, field trips, etc.) to illustrate useful ways to get rid of trash.
- cutting down on our garbage
- compacting trash into building materials
- using it for landfill
- burning it and using the heat for energy.

BUSY BOTTLE

WHAT IS IT

a container......
an old cookie jar
is great. It's a
jar with various
activities to add
lots of zest to
routine chores

OR

to distract kids
from unacceptable
behavior

OR

give children
different house
keeping experiences

OR

give parents a
break....rah, rah !!

BUSY BOTTLE RULE:

You need to do the
activity that is
drawn. No "put-backs"
or "draw-overs !!"

Brush your teeth for one minute and smile.

Water the lawn.

Help pop a pan of popcorn for an after dinner snack.

WHAT TO DO

Take twenty to thirty
pieces of paper and
write in the activities
that are applicable to
your child(ren).

Have your preschooler help
with the ideas to insure
enthusiastic participation.

Fold up the strips and put
them in the Busy Bottle.
You may want to change
them from time to time.

Your Busy Bottle is ready
and waiting for the right
situation.

Find three snails or bugs.

Give mom or dad a backrub.

BUSY BOTTLE

SANITY SAVER

Make a sandwich for lunch.

Hang up 5 garments.

Hold and love your pet for three minutes. Scratch fleas, too!

Peel and eat an orange.

Fix one toy.

Take out the garbage.

Draw a picture to be given to _____ (name).

Skip to _____ and back.

Shake two throwrugs.

Sing a song to your parent.

Set the table for the next meal.

Unplug the toaster... clean and shine.

"UNFUNS"

For those chores that EVERYONE hates to do, BUT that have to be done, whip up an Un-fun jar.

Un-funs are "do together jobs"... like making the bunk bed, sorting the wash, washing off finger prints, etc.

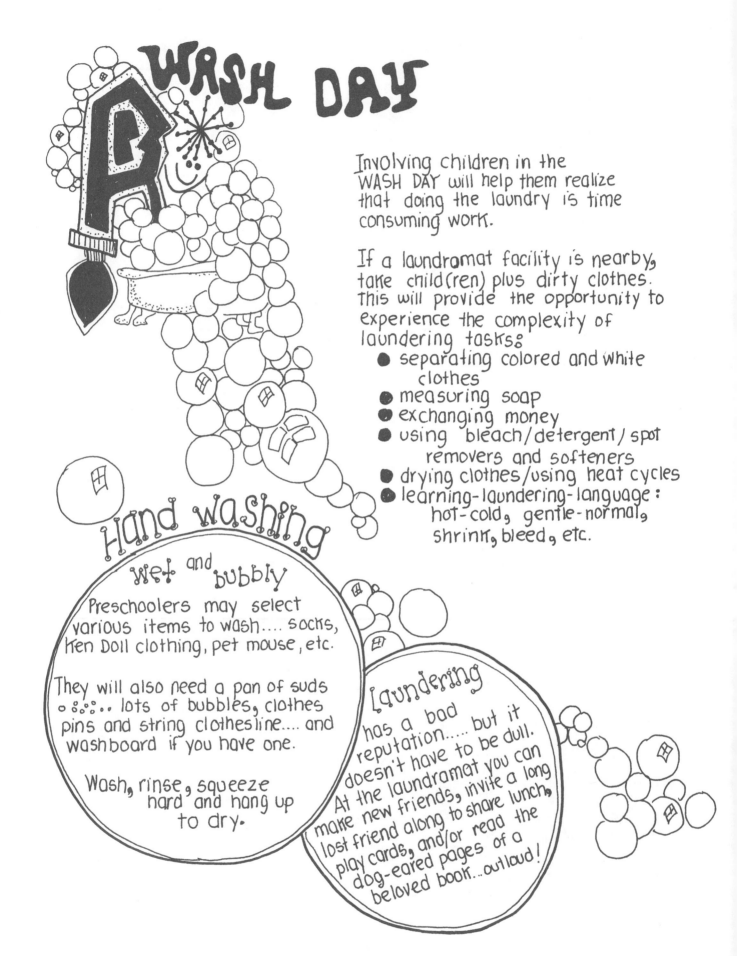

WASH DAY

Involving children in the WASH DAY will help them realize that doing the laundry is time consuming work.

If a laundromat facility is nearby, take child(ren) plus dirty clothes. This will provide the opportunity to experience the complexity of laundering tasks:
- separating colored and white clothes
- measuring soap
- exchanging money
- using bleach/detergent/spot removers and softeners
- drying clothes/using heat cycles
- learning-laundering-language: hot-cold, gentle-normal, shrink, bleed, etc.

Hand washing

wet and bubbly

Preschoolers may select various items to wash.... socks, Ken Doll clothing, pet mouse, etc.

They will also need a pan of suds ᵒ ° ᵒ ° .. lots of bubbles, clothes pins and string clothesline.... and washboard if you have one.

Wash, rinse, squeeze hard and hang up to dry.

Laundering

has a bad reputation..... but it doesn't have to be dull. At the laundramat you can make new friends, invite a long lost friend along to share lunch, play cards, and/or read the dog-eared pages of a beloved book...outloud!

SOAP

Water can lead to all sorts of cleaning and beautification adventures.

PAINTING the house with water

BLOWING bubbles

LEARNING about floating and non-floating objects

DEVELOPING cooperative play by sharing dish duty with a friend

WATCHING water disappear as the sun absorbs the moisture.

END PRODUCT one clean kid!

Arrange to do your wash at the laundramat during evening or weekend hours when many males clean their dirties. Discuss that everyone needs his/her clothes cleaned..... adults and children/ females and males.

check all pockets please

FOLDING

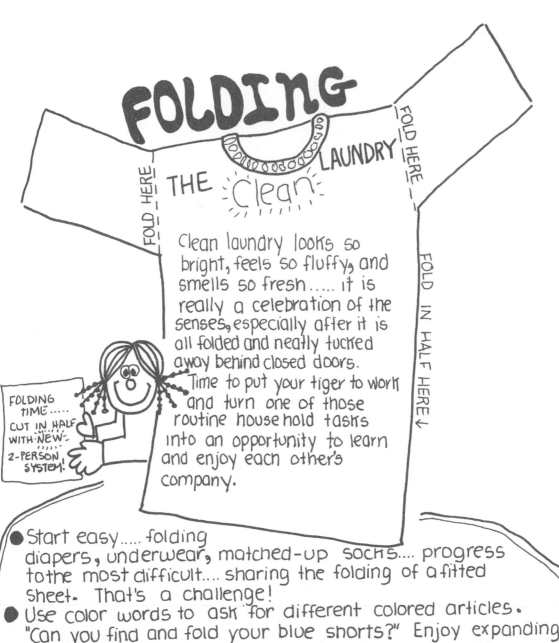

FOLD HERE · **FOLD HERE**

THE :Clean: LAUNDRY

FOLD IN HALF HERE ↓

Clean laundry looks so bright, feels so fluffy, and smells so fresh..... it is really a celebration of the senses, especially after it is all folded and neatly tucked away behind closed doors.
Time to put your tiger to work and turn one of those routine household tasks into an opportunity to learn and enjoy each other's company.

FOLDING TIME.....
CUT IN HALF WITH NEW 2-PERSON SYSTEM!

● Start easy..... folding diapers, underwear, matched-up socks.... progress to the most difficult.... sharing the folding of a fitted sheet. That's a challenge!

● Use color words to ask for different colored articles. "Can you find and fold your blue shorts?" Enjoy expanding language skills.

● Sorting folded clean clothes (or dirty ones) provides an excellent opportunity to learn and practice classification skills.

● Let your preschooler(s) put things in piles— brother, mom, sister, dad, towels, etc. Out of curiosity, who has the biggest stack? Why?

● How many folded towels can your child stack before the towels topple over?

● Put a sock on your preschooler's hand. Name it Ms. Sandy-Smoother or Mr. Freddy-Flat-Folder and and you have a puppet to help fold.

Helping Father (or Mother or Brother or Sister)

I help my Dad
I sweep the floor ......(swing arms, pretending to sweep),

I dust the table ......(make a circular motion with one hand),

I run to the store ......(run a few steps and then run back),

I help him beat eggs ...(hold hands together, moving one in
                     a small circle),
And sift flour for cakes .(hold one hand closed, shake it
                     back and forth),
Then I help him eat......(hold hand to lips, pretend to eat),
All the good things we make.

Sing a song to the tune of "Here We Go 'Round the Mulberry Bush" to demonstrate all the skills involved in keeping a full drawer of work/play clothes.

Monday: This is the way we wash our clothes,
Wash our clothes, wash our clothes,
This is the way we wash our clothes,
So early on Monday morning.
(Repeat, using:)

Tuesday: Fold our clothes
Wednesday: Iron our clothes
Thursday: Put them away
Friday: Sew our clothes
Saturday: Play in our clothes
Sunday: Get dressed up in our clothes

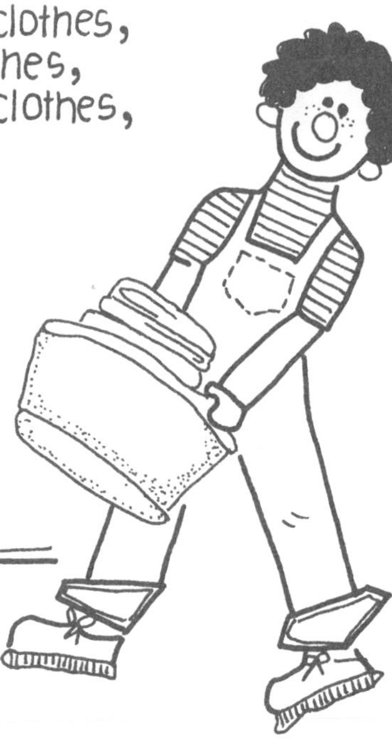

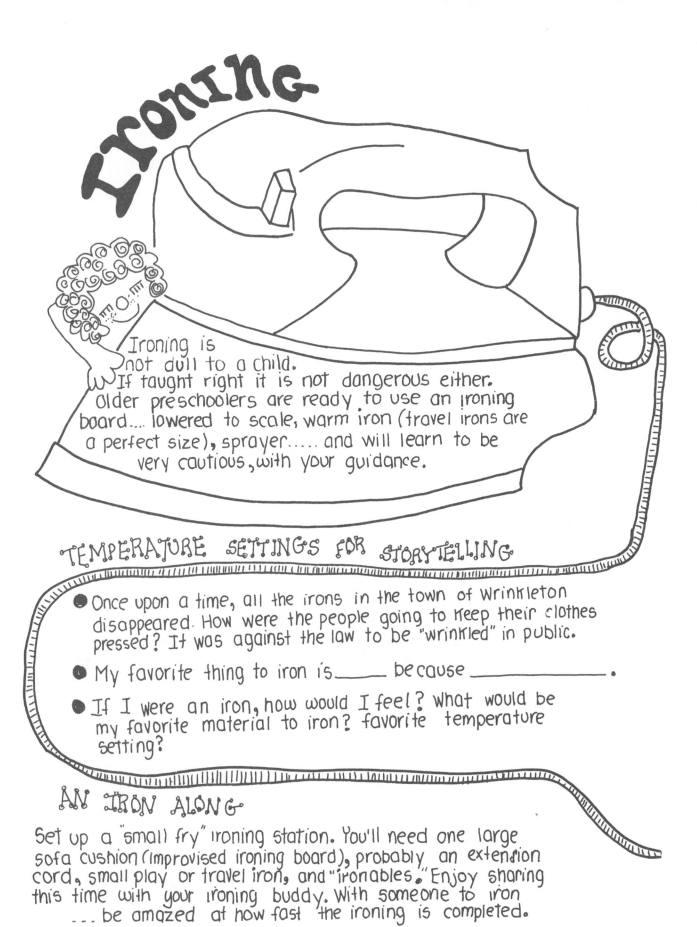

Ironing

Ironing is not dull to a child. If taught right it is not dangerous either. Older preschoolers are ready to use an ironing board.... lowered to scale, warm iron (travel irons are a perfect size), sprayer..... and will learn to be very cautious, with your guidance.

TEMPERATURE SETTINGS FOR STORYTELLING

- Once upon a time, all the irons in the town of Wrinkleton disappeared. How were the people going to keep their clothes pressed? It was against the law to be "wrinkled" in public.

- My favorite thing to iron is ____ because _____.

- If I were an iron, how would I feel? What would be my favorite material to iron? favorite temperature setting?

AN IRON ALONG

Set up a "small fry" ironing station. You'll need one large sofa cushion (improvised ironing board), probably an extension cord, small play or travel iron, and "ironables." Enjoy sharing this time with your ironing buddy. With someone to iron ...be amazed at how fast the ironing is completed.

While you are ironing, children can be working on an ironing art piece. Provide a work area covered with "lots" of newspaper; include old crayons, waxed paper and a potato peeler. AT first, help shave chips of crayons on to a piece of waxed paper; then let the "kids" experiment with color and design while you iron.

Take a break and assist in the completion of an ironed art picture.

Be sure and cover the crayon chips with another piece of waxed paper; lay a towel over that and press with a <u>warm</u> iron.

Have your child(ren) select colorful patches and iron them on holes in pants.

PATCHES

IRON~ONS

- You'll need crayons, an old t-shirt, and a <u>warm</u> iron.
- Design: write a silly saying or have your preschooler(s) draw a self-portrait, name, etc.
- Be sure to have the child(ren) press hard on the crayons.
- The ironing should be supervised.
- Leave the crayoned side up.
- Slide pieces of paper between the board and shirt and the iron.
- Instruct the ironer to press slowly, giving the crayon enough heat to melt and impregnate the cloth.
- Crayons are brighter after melting.
- Wash in <u>cold</u> water.

Visit your local dry cleaners. Watch the professionals and their heavy duty equipment. Notice the intensity of heat and hard work involved in pressing each garment. Talk about the working conditions, skills and costs.

SEWING

Although most preschoolers are too young to mend their own clothing or to sew on buttons, they are not too young to begin to learn some sewing fundamentals. Learning sewing skills may help to alleviate the helpless adult who is baffled by a missing button, a torn pocket, etc.

While you are mending or sewing, introduce "kids" to sewing by assisting them in starting their projects:

- Put together a sewing box of discards..... ribbon, buttons, lace, pockets, appliques, pieces of loosely woven material.... a large needle and thread.

- Thread a big needle with sturdy thread. Tie a knot in one end so that the thread does not keep coming out. Demonstrate the "in and out" stitch.

- Buttons 'N Laces - assorted buttons and laces to use in stringing, sorting and counting (CC)

PASTA JEWELRY
(pre-sewing activity)

You'll need pasta with large holes, cut straws, and any other stringing material, such as a piece of yarn with a tip taped to make it strong.

Tie on the first macaroni. Pre-schoolers delight in one-at-a-time stringing and pride in wearing their creation. Preschool boys and girls enjoy wearing jewelry.... especially when they can say.... LOOK, I MADE IT MYSELF !!!

SEWING CARDS

- Use plastic darning needles with yarn on burlap squares. Be sure to knot the end of the yarn.

- Create your own sewing cards with thin cardboard and a paper punch.

- Glue colorful non-sexist magazine pictures to cardboard and punch holes an inch apart.

- Use a shoe string to sew.

- Keep these ready for a sewing session. Old greeting cards also make interesting sewing cards.

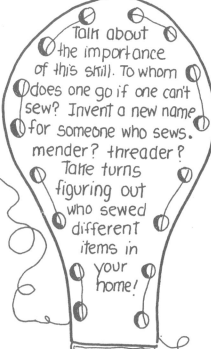

Talk about the importance of this skill. To whom does one go if one can't sew? Invent a new name for someone who sews. mender? threader? Take turns figuring out who sewed different items in your home!

HIDE THE THIMBLE

Hide a thimble and send your preschoolers scurrying to find it. Give clues such as "You're getting warm" as they approach it and "cold" as they are going away from it.

Variation: Use this activity to practice "following directions," such as...... take five steps forward; look under the pillow.

This game can be used to familiarize children with names of sewing supplies, eg., pinking shears, measuring tape, pin cushion, snaps, hooks and eyes, etc. Talk about the function of each item before it is hidden.

READ... PETER LEARNS TO CROCHET by Irene Levinson
Peter finally finds someone to teach
him how to crochet. (NSP)

MEAL PREPARATION

A FAMILY THAT COOKS TOGETHER STAYS TOGETHER

- menu planning
- shopping
- unbagging
- cooking
- setting up
- cleaning up

Meal preparation is probably the most important job in the "whole wide world"•••• and if one thinks about it, one of the most complex. Meal Preparation involves learning to select, purchase, prepare, cook and serve food •••• a shared family responsibility.

THE PURPOSES OF THIS SECTION ARE TO:

- familiarize preschoolers with the complexities of meal preparation

- provide activities to experience meal preparation skills -- we believe in learning by doing

- and, relate the skills to jobs outside the home and ones with which preschoolers are familiar so that they will gain an understanding and respect for the persons who do them in the home

THINK about all the time consuming, but easy things involved with meal preparation that an adult usually does... like folding napkins, grating cheese, etc. WHY not let a child try some of these?

Realistically, it will take more of your TIME and EFFORT and ATTENTION to provide opportunities for children to practice these meal preparation skills. But the time and energy invested will be rewarded by children beginning to REALLY help.

And you can be helped, too. You can change routine activities in which preschoolers can often be hinderances into entertaining learning experiences.

But, most importantly, you can help preschoolers become self-reliant and competent in this living skill.

135

MEAL PREPARATION AWARENESS ACTIVITIES

things we can do ✓

☐ <u>Start</u> with an afternoon adventure to a favorite restaurant (during its slow hours, please). <u>Ask</u> to see the kitchen.... the gigantic stoves, ovens, dishwasher, refrigerators, etc. <u>Talk</u> about the many steps required to put the meal you are enjoying on the table. <u>Compare</u> restaurant meals to family ones.

☐ Pretend you are opening a family restaurant. Discuss the things you'd have to do.... whew!!! and who would do them... cooks, cleaners, etc.

☐ Play a game: who does it? What do they do?

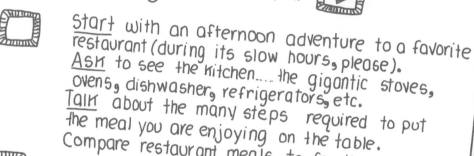

"At home"	"In a restaurant"	"Occupation"
Planning meals......	Budgeting.........	Manager / cook
Grocery shopping....	Purchasing........	Sales / Manager
Putting away........	Storing...........	Kitchen help
Cooking..	Preparing.........	Cook
Setting table.......	Serving...........	Waiters and waitresses
and serving		
Washing up........	Cleaning up........	Bus girl/boy
and putting away		Dishwasher

Who is responsible for these jobs in the home? in your home?

☐ Other...............

CUT AND PASTE MENU

Before marketing, make a "cut and paste" picture menu together. Cut pictures from magazines; talk about nutritious foods and suggest including one food from each food group. Example...... "For lunch today, can you find a fruit you'd like to eat?" For younger preschoolers, precut an assortment of pictures.

Shop for the meal together.

GROCERY LIST

Draw a picture shopping list and you're off. By four, a preschooler probably has the local market wired and will delight in filling up the shopping cart. Keep it simple. Start with "unbreakable" basic items like cat food, cereal, soap, canned foods. Ask the grocer to bag these items separately. While you are putting away the family groceries, your companion shopper will put away his/her bag of groceries.

Take some extra time on market day and explore the "life" behind the scenes of a super market.

The average person eats 3 lbs. of food each day; that's 21 lbs. a week or 1,097 lbs./year.

OR, for a 4-person family.....that's 84 lbs. of food a week.
(Allison, 1976)

THE FUSSIES

Many preschoolers are infamous for being fussy eaters. They often base their likes and dislikes on the way food looks. One day they'll love it; the next day they'll hate it. To keep up with that tyrant in the kitchen, try one of the following "fussy" activities:

Use unusual cookie cutters for a variety of sandwich shapes... a Bugs Bunny open-faced carrot eared hamburger is irresistable and nutritious.

How about a "hungry caterpillar"... bread circles with different sandwich spreads on each circle (cream cheese, peanut butter, ham spread, etc.)? Decorate each open-faced circle differently with carrot curls, sesame seeds, sprouts, olives, pickles, etc. Creepy crawlers are best served to friends and enjoyed together.

Read... BREAD AND JAM FOR FRANCES by Russell Haban. Frances finally gets tired of just eating bread and jam.

PRESENTED PROPERLY,

MOST NUTRITIONAL MEALS CAN BE AN EXCITING ADVENTURE

For a "grinning" brown-bagger's treat .....cut an orange slice small enough to stay in his/her mouth. Draw teeth on with a felt pen. Make a few extra sets of play teeth for friends. Wrap in plastic. Pack in lunch.

- How about a progressive lunch or scavenger food hunt? Prearrange this activity with your neighborhood friends.

- Draw a picture scavenger hunt list. Suggestions: banana, box of raisins, green vegetable, circle shaped meat, etc.

lunch list
box raisins
2 kumquats
5 pickles

- Furnish a brown paper bag. Meet back at home to enjoy munching a lunch.

How about a box lunch !!!

Wrap each food item in brightly colored party paper.

Maybe a treasure hunt to find wrapped sandwich, fruit and drink in the backyard or family room.

← look here

Hike in the House

To combat boredom or a rainy day and/or to solve a fussy eater situation, plan a hike through the house pretending you are all outside in the woods. Walk around the RIVER (couch), under the BRIDGE (table), up the side of the MOUNTAIN (stairs), etc. After lunch, "hike" back with trash in bag. Talk about litter bugs and leaving "campsite" clean.

Read LET'S EAT by Gyo Fujikawa

Plan a picnic or spontaneous party to celebrate some unusual event... Ground Hog Day, Count-to-10-Day, Dressed Myself Day, etc.

Celebrate with colored (crayoned) paper plates and cups, party hats and straws.

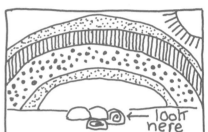

COOKING is a life skill that requires knowledge of:
- math
- safety
- science
- language
- hygiene
- nutrition
- aesthetics.

Cooking is intrinsically exciting... children love to do things they see their parents do. IT IS REAL and great to be able to "see" and "eat" the finished product.

Women are most often the ones perceived of by children as cooks; boys are often denied the pleasures and learning that cooking brings. This section will help to reinforce the feeling that cooking is a life skill...

"all people need"

IN YOUR FAMILY......
who cooks:
...for company?
....on weekends?
....on vacation?
....daily?

take a bite
and
grow!

THE FORTUNATE
CATASTROPHE
A rat family leads a
stereotypic life style until
the day of the catastrophe.
Parents are forced to
switch roles.
by Adela Turin
Nella Bosnia (WRPC)

read

Dad,
if you regularly
are unable to do so,
treat the family to your
cooking experiments at
least once a week....
for company.....

...restaurants
with male/female
chefs. or tune into one
of the T.V. cooking shows.
Check for ones with
female chefs. Chefs with
higher status have
been traditionally
reserved for
males.

visit

role play

Martin's Father.
Martin spends a day
with his dad, doing the
laundry, playing games,
etc. Enjoyable story
to act out! by
Margrit
Eichler (LP)

HOW TO START

Kid Lib

1. LEARN SAFETY PRECAUTIONS

- Wash hands before starting.
- Wear adult t-shirt for protection.
- Use one bowl....rinsing and reusing.

2. PRACTICE SIMPLE COOKING SKILLS

- scrubbing vegetables with a brush
- tearing, breaking, and snapping vegetables
- wrapping bread dough on a stick
- peeling eggs or corn on the cob
- mixing jello
- cracking raw eggs (a favorite)
- beating with an egg beater
- cutting with a dull knife; try bananas as a starter

3. TASTE WITH YOUR TODDLER

Ask?
Is taste linked more to sight or smell?

- You'll need some bite-sized pieces of food that are all crunchy in the same way, like apples, carrot, onion, raw carrot, turnip, etc.
- Close eyes and hold nose.
- Let your preschooler put something in your mouth. Guess what it is.
- Then switch so your child can explore his/her tasting sense.
- Variations:
  Creamy things....ice cream, sour cream, yogurt, pudding, mashed potatoes, etc.

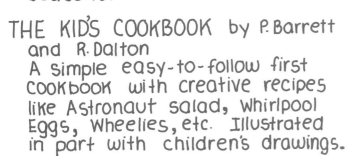

4. SELECT SIMPLE RECIPES!

LOVE AT FIRST BITE by Jane Cooper
A delightfully illustrated easy-to-follow cookbook of over 150 "no bake" quick recipes. Includes how to make your own yogurt, potato chips, granola, etc. Also, it describes kitchen utensils and presents cooking terminology.

A CHILD'S COOKBOOK by Bev Veitch, Thelma Harms, Tia Wallace, Gerry Wallace
This book centers around cooking, learning techiques and rationale. It is a single portion recipe book– cleverly illustrated and hand-lettered. (656 Terra California Drive #3, Walnut Creek, CA 94595.... to order direct)

KIDS ARE NATURAL COOKS by Parents' Nursery School Cambridge, Mass. Houghton Mifflin
Great book for beginning cooks to use at home, especially for those who believe in "natural" foods. Recipes are arranged by seasons.

THE KID'S COOKBOOK by P. Barrett and R. Dalton
A simple easy-to-follow first cookbook with creative recipes like Astronaut salad, Whirlpool Eggs, Wheelies, etc. Illustrated in part with children's drawings.

COOKING AND EATING WITH CHILDREN by McAfee, Haines, Young
This book is aimed at children who are expected to share all cooking tasks equally. It centers around experiences children can get from cooking and eating together.

COOKING RECIPES

NON-SEXIST COOKERY
by the yum yum kids

1. easy•to•do first adventures

● popsicles= pour juices in ice cube trays.
● ice cream sandwiches= scoop a tablespoon of ice cream, put between 2 cookies....freeze.
● frozen yogurt bars= pour yogurt into ice cube trays....freeze.
● fill•er•up = celery with peanut butter, sprinkle on nuts or coconuts.

2. press•your•lunch Ironed Sandwich

● Cut one slice of bread in half.
● Butter on one side only.
● Take one piece of cheese and make a sandwich with buttered sides out.
● Fold foil over sandwich.
● Iron "lightly" on both sides until cheese melts and bread is brown. (veitch, et al., 1977)

3. Sandwich faces

● Cut a circle from bread with a glass....then
● spread wheat bread with cream cheese or peanut butter.
● gather up various foods for decorations...parsley, grated carrots, olives, sprouts, etc.
● have your preschooler look in a mirror and make his/her face with the decorations. (veitch, et al., 1977)

4. my child(ren)'s favorite cooking adventures are:

● _____
● _____
● _____
● _____

FAMILY · SANDWICH

COMBINE

SPREADS

- mustard
- mayonnaise
- catsup
- "stinky" mustard
- horseradish
- taco sauce

THE HEAVIES

- chicken
- ham
- tuna
- salami
- eggs

CHEESES

- you name it!

VEGIES

- lettuce
- tomato
- sprouts
- mushrooms

EXTRAS

- cucumber slices
- olives
- onions
- avocado

GO FOR IT!

- peanut butter
- bananas
- raisins
- cream cheese

5. For the layered-look in non-sexist cooking, try a family sandwich. The whole family or gathering can be involved.

Set the table picnic style. Slice a loaf of Italian bread in half and layer away. Put the "extras" on top of the "spreads;" they will keep them from slipping out. Slice the layered loaf sandwich into smaller sandwiches and

BON APPETITE!

HOW DID THE "SANDWICH" GET ITS NAME?

According to legend, the sandwich was invented in England, 1700's, by the Fourth Earl of Sandwich. This gambling man once refused to leave the gametable for over 24 hours. Ignoring calls to dinner, he ordered a servant to bring him meat placed between two slices of buttered bread and he kept right on playing. (Cooper, 1977)

145

KITCHEN KOOKIES

"i did it"!!! the world's longest liver-------flavored noodle!!!

"unofficial" world records

- Did you know that william Allen set the "unofficial" world record for broom balancing? 1 hour, 15 minutes!
- To add enjoyment to a dreaded living skill activity, INVENT a "world record" contest centering around the household job.
- Why not send your "record" to the Guinness Book of World Records? Be sure to have confirmation of a newspaper and witness affidavit.

UNOFFICIAL RECORDS WAITING TO BE SET....

- How many noodles can be stacked in a tablespoon?
- How much weight can you gain in one day from your own experimental cooking?
- How many pairs of folded socks can you stack on top of each other?
- How high (inches) can you rake a pile of leaves in Arizona?

NON-SEXIST PET

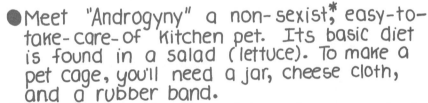

- Meet "Androgyny" a non-sexist,* easy-to-take-care-of kitchen pet. Its basic diet is found in a salad (lettuce). To make a pet cage, you'll need a jar, cheese cloth, and a rubber band.
- Find a snail (you might have to go on a night hunt), put it in a jar, secure cheese cloth over the top with the rubber band.
- Daily....rinse out her/his cage and feed.
- Watch closely and you can see it gnaw away.
- Please don't leave it in the sun. It sunburns easily!
- Take it on a walk. Place your pet on a black piece of paper. What type of trail does it leave?

    * A snail is both sexes in one shell ... a hermaphrodite ... but it does need another snail to reproduce.

MY Name is Androgyny

EGG·CEPTIONALLY·CELLENT·TIVITIES

Teach your preschooler(s) this trick. Say... Do you think you can crush a raw egg with one hand? The trick: Hold an egg in the palm of your hand with fingers wrapped around it. Try to crush it. It won't break. The reason: the pressure put on the egg is evenly distributed by a "cupped" hand.

EGGSTRA STRONG?

I'm cracking up!!!

It's kitchen magic....present this kitchen trick to your child(ren). You'll need:

> 3 tbsps. alum (from drugstore)
> 1 cup vinegar
> a small brush

Dissolve the alum into the vinegar and use the solution to draw (or adults to write) on a "very fresh" egg. After the egg has completely dried, boil it in water for 15 minutes. When egg is peeled, the drawing will have transferred to the egg. (Nice way to include "love" messages in lunches.)

TO TEST AN EGG FOR FRESHNESS, PLACE IT IN A DEEP GLASS OF WATER.

● If it stands on end or floats... throw it out !!!

● If the large end rises slightly, it's a little stale.

● If it sinks and lies on its side... it's fresh.

147

THE SET UP

WHAT'S IN THE KITCHEN? Play this memory game.
Learning to look is an important "brain" exercise.
"Noticing" helps us to see things we tend to ignore.
Imagine you are in the kitchen. What is usually
on the table? on the counter? in the refrigerator?
Take turns remembering all the things you can,
then go and see how much your mind's eye
has remembered.

PLACEMATS   Make your own
Most supermarkets have plain paper placemats.
Trace the shapes of kitchenware that you will
need for this meal with crayon or felt pens.
Before mealtime, take out the items that are
needed and ZIP.....your child(ren) can match shapes.

"TALKING" CENTERPIECES
"Turn the table" on an often hurried, sometimes
problem-producing mealtime with something
unique to talk about.
Make a family tree. Display several family
photos on a tree branch.
Have your preschooler select 3 or 4 of his/her
favorite possessions and arrange for decorations.
Jointly, make an edible centerpiece sculpture.
include favorite fruits, cheeses, nuts, etc. Play
what's missing. Use the "edible-talkable." One
person removes one item s/he would like for
dessert, while others keep their eyes shut and
and guess what has been selected.... perfect
way to serve dessert.

THE CLEAN UP

RULES

- Each person is responsible for his/her own eating ware.
- Carry one item at a time.
- No stacking please.

NON-SEXIST SOFTENER ~and~ SOAP

GUARANTEED EQUAL

- Even if you have a dishwasher, with a little pre-thought, this water play activity will be a perfect chance to catch a moment of rest.
- For an accident-free activity, wash and dry all the breakable dishes and glasses plus sharp knives.
- Bring over a chair to stand on and plastic bib to "somewhat" water proof the activity.
- Set up one sink for washing....the other for rinsing.
- Measure soap together... submerge eatingware.
- Demonstrate how to rub a <u>small</u> sponge over all sides of the washables.
- Rinse and put in drainer.
- Enjoy your second cup of coffee, glass of wine or evening paper

Is dishwashing a hassle. or problem in your liberated household? READ
   <u>The Man who Didn't Wash His Dishes</u> (Phyllis Krasilovsky)
The children's book is about a man who loves to cook, but hates to clean up .... and his solution to this catch-22.

HOME MAINTENANCE

There always seems to be little "fix-it" or "clean-up" jobs to be done around or outside the home that can be a real nuisance or can be fun energy-releasers that when done can provide for a feeling of accomplishment.

Traditionally, the male of the household has been called upon by the female to do these jobs, yet many females could do them.

Home maintenance skills can be learned by BOTH girls and boys, even if at a very rudimentary level. This may mean learning through observation and by having procedures and tools explained than actually "learning by doing."

ACTIVITIES

The following activities are ones which could be done by women—to provide a non-traditional role model, and/or by men with young girls and/or boys. The importance of providing a role model cannot be overstressed.

- tightening something that is loose
- using nuts and bolts, washers, screwdrivers, wrenches
- fixing leaky faucets or other simple plumbing chores
- gluing something
- cleaning out the garage
- hammering nails
- fixing the broken toys
- changing fuses and lightbulbs
- painting furniture, walls, fences
- sandpapering a weathered, worn, or rough wood surface

If you are female think of the maintenance jobs you have usually asked a male to do for you. Could you learn to do some of these by yourself? What models are you providing for your child?

RESOURCES

Tinker Tools (Child Guidance)
Take Apart Tool Box (Child Guidance)
Truck'n Tool Kit (Kusan)
old tools/box, broken appliances, etc.

BOOKS FOR ADULTS

RECIPES FOR HOME REPAIR by Alvin Ubell and Sam Bittman

I TOOK A HAMMER IN MY HAND "The woman's build-it and fix-it hand book" by Florence Adams

AGAINST THE GRAIN by Dale McCormick (ICWP)

A WOMAN'S GUIDE TO THE CARE AND FEEDING OF AN AUTOMOBILE by Carmel Berman Rheingold

MANUAL FOR HOME REPAIRS, REMODELING AND MAINTENANCE by Grosset and Dunlap Publishers

YARDWORK

- sweeping
- mowing
- watering
- weeding
- planting
- picking flowers
- using tools
- bug patrol

Traditionally, gardening and yard maintenance have been delegated to the male in a family. There is the mental image of Dad pushing the lawnmower on Saturday.

The earth and nature provide a positive environment for children....it's like no-fault insurance. Children seem born with a willingness and a desire to love anything that's alive.

Yardwork teaches children yard maintenance and gardening skills. They can learn to distinguish "good" vs. "bad" (weed, poisonous plants, etc), how things grow, and the relationship of water, sun and soil. When children feel a part of nature, it is easier for them to sort out their place in it.

Yardwork is a "natural" type of living skill to teach both boys and girls.

ACTIVITIES

- sweep patio, sidewalks
- pull weeds
- rake leaves
- water plants with hose
- control bugs
- pick up stones out of garden
- snip off old flowers
- fill bird feeders
- pick ripe fruit and vegetables
- scoop up animal poop with small shovel

BOOKS

THE KIDS' GARDEN BOOK
by Patricia Pelrich

Book for older preschoolers. Special features include: garbage gardening, terrariums, learning to plant, plus growing plants in water and making a park for a turtle.

GROWING UP GREEN: PARENTS AND CHILDREN GARDENING TOGETHER
by Skelsey and Huckaby

For the family. Explores all aspects of gardening from growing pumpkin seeds to wind, weather, trees, and birds.... to gardening from seeds... to harvest.... to spider webs... and pressing flowers.

TOOLS

Teach the most efficient way to use gardening tools.
- hoe
- hose
- rake
- broom
- shovel
- watering can
- plastic pots
- bucket
- lawn mower

G.U.E. MOTORS

WEEDING

Show preschoolers what weeds look like. (A weed is an undesirable plant; possibly to a child there are no weeds.) Pull weeds out often-- they use up food and space your plants need.

Plants also need sunshine, food from the soil and water to grow.
Farming tools: rake, hoe and shovel (cc)

WATERING

A good sign that plants need watering is a diagnosed case of the "droops." Dressed properly in their "swim or birthday suits, preschoolers are born water-experts. Be sure to close all windows and doors to the house. Demonstrate the finger-moisture test (stick "pointer" finger in the soil.... if dry → water). Watering techniques include:

- "slow drizzle" method
- the flash flood
- the soaker (Soak pot in a bucket of water. Plant knows when to stop drinking.)
- misting
- ice cube dripless method (6/6" pot)

PLANTING

NEEDED: one half day of ☼ and dark, rich well-drained soil. Buy bedding plants for best results. Let preschooler(s) select an interesting array of plants or seeds. Suggest onions, garlic, and marigold to keep the bugs away. Plant as directed. Preschoolers cannot and should not be expected to be as attentive to their gardens as are adults.

Do you have cracks in your sidewalks? Let your kid(s) plant them with seeds. Rake the soil with a fork and plant. Nasturtium are great in salads and fast growers, too.

GARLIC

NON-SEXIST SOIL

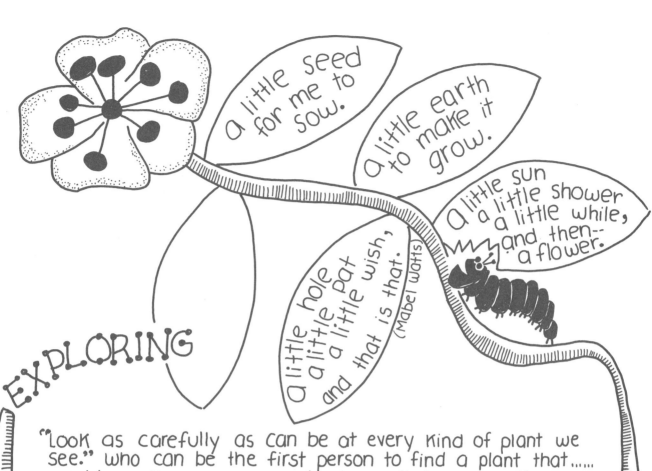

A little seed for me to sow.

A little earth to make it grow.

A little sun a little shower a little while, and then-- a flower.

A little hole a little pat a little wish, and that is that.
(Mabel Watts)

EXPLORING

"Look as carefully as can be at every kind of plant we see." Who can be the first person to find a plant that......would make you say ouch....., can climb....., hugs the ground..... has a flower like a bush..... has leaves like needles....., has leaves bigger than your hand?

Take a backyard hike and practice nature's language. For older preschoolers go on an ABC HIKE. Take turns looking for items in alphabetical order.... e.g. A-ant, B-bush, C-cocoon, etc. Nature's language---- leaves, trees, shrubs, wildflowers, birds, nests, animal tracks, seeds, insects, butterflies, flowers, etc.

Talk about the parts of a plant....... the root, stem, leaves, seed, flower and fruit. What can a person eat from a plant?

ROOT........carrot, radish, onion, potato
STEM........celery, asparagus
LEAVES....cabbage, lettuce, spinach
FRUITS....apple, pear, banana
SEEDS.....corn, beans, wheat, peas
FLOWERS.broccoli, cauliflower

READ... PLANTS IN WINTER by Joanna Cole

BUG PATROL

GO "BUGGY" WITH YOUR PRESCHOOLER

Plants usually do not like bugs. Organize a bug patrol and construct some bug cages. Your plants are probably "gourmet delights" to the local insect population. Some people spray plants with chemicals to keep bugs away. This is BAD NEWS since birds can die if they eat poisoned plants or bugs. Snails and caterpillars can be fed to the birds. Let your preschooler try beer, marigolds or night hikes...first...to rid your garden of unwanted creepy crawlers.

READ

WE LIKE BUGS by Gladys Conklin
All different kinds of bugs... non-sexist, girls involved with bugs. Best with older preschoolers.

THE VERY HUNGRY CATERPILLAR by Eric Carle
Large colorful drawings illustrate the life cycle of a butterfly.

PRETEND TO BE A CHIRPER, LEAPER, FLYER, OR CREEPER.

Home sweet Home

Two eat food cans and a piece of wire screen can be assembled for a bug "home."

I WONDER WHY, MY PARENTS THINK THAT FINDERS CAN'T BE KEEPERS!

more LIVING SKILLS resources...

KATY ROSE IS MAD by Carol Nicklaus
Katy would rather play baseball than clean her room.

RAFIKI by Nora Langner
Rafiki's arrival in the jungle helps the animals learn role reversals and that it is <u>not</u> true that "only girls do housework."

THE COUNTRY BUNNY AND THE LITTLE GOLD SHOES
by Dubose Heyward and Marjory Zarssoni
While a mother rabbit carries out her duties as a strong and proud Easter Bunny, her bunnies-both female and male- take care of the house.

WHY COULDN'T I BE AN ONLY KID LIKE YOU, WIGGER?
by Barbara Shook Hazen. Gripes about living in a large family with illustrations of boys doing housework and taking care of babies.

A TERRIBLE THING HAPPENED AT OUR HOUSE by Marge Blaine
The children and their father learn what it takes to keep a family functioning when the mother returns to work as a science teacher.

AMANDA THE PANDA AND THE REDHEAD by Susan Terris
The father and mother both take care of their children and the house.

EVAN'S CORNER by Elizabeth Starr Hill
Evan's older sister and father help take care of the children as his mother works.

HEALTH & CHILD CARE

HEALTH & CHILD CARE

• first aid
• safety
• nutrition

The "bump club," band aid magic, and safety patrol are everyday happenings for a homemaker and others who interact with preschoolers. Adults who care for children usually have acquired health care skills:
• knowledge of first aid techniques
• understanding of safety precautions
• caring for the sick
• understanding of the relationship between food and good health.

BOOKS

A HOSPITAL IS WHERE   by Grace Smith
The perfect gift for a hospital-
bound preschooler. This book
contains children's pictures and
words about being in the hospital
with spaces for a child to add
her/his feelings.

DIANA AND HER RHINOCEROS
by Edward Ardizzone
A young girl takes care of
a sick rhinoceros.

A SIGH OF RELIEF...."the first-aid handbook for childhood emergencies"
Produced by Martin I. Green
"Fast, simple instructions for every
childhood illness and injury; and
how to prevent accidents from
happening." Home safety and toy
safety are of particular
interest. Be sure to
substitute s/he in place
of he.

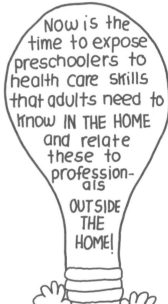

Now is the
time to expose
preschoolers to
health care skills
that adults need to
know IN THE HOME
and relate
these to
profession-
als

OUTSIDE
THE
HOME!

children
at
play

BAND AID MAGIC

Children like band aids. They not only keep a wound clean, they are also "magic." Take the time to assemble a child's first aid box. Put it in an easy-to-reach place for your child(ren) ....maybe under the bathroom sink.

FIRST AID BOX

- box for supplies...mark ✚ on top
- ouchless band aids, various shapes
- soap and cottonballs for cleaning "owies"
- sharpie pens (optional) for drawing ☺ on band aids

An easy-to-reach first aid box can help set the scene for this magic show. Next time you personally need a band aid, let your preschooler take over. You'll be amazed at her/his expertise. Children enjoy the satisfaction of taking care of their own "owies."

One suggestion is to limit the number of band aids in the first aid box......or one day you might find your child's bedroom transformed into a hospital....with all the stuffed-animal patients fully bandaged and one empty box of band aids.

me fell off my bike and put band aid on my nose.
while running, I tripped, now have 2 on my toes.
me played with my dog and he bit my bottom
8 band aids now... when I sit I know I've got 'em.
3 on my wrist, where I was hit by a ball.
And 4 on my ankle where I fall in the hall.
while hitting the hammer on my pail,
I now have one on each finger nail.
5 on my shoulder when I fell off the swing,
2 on my elbows 'though I don't feel a thing.
me find BIG BOX with 50 more,
too bad, I don't have space for cuts or sore.
today I think is not my day,
I should have stayed home
And not gone out to play.   by Gandoff

BURNS

Preschoolers can learn burn first aid. Here are 3 ways to stop burns from hurting.

- The quickest is putting the burned area under the cold water tap.
- Try an aloe plant which can be found in most nurseries. Cut off a piece of the peel and squeeze the juice on the burn.
- Mix baking soda with water to make a paste. Smooth great gobs of it over the burned area. Reapply the thin paste if the pain continues.

STINGS

"I'm taking home a baby bumble bee won't my parents be so proud of me.... OUCH! It bit me."
QUICK.... fetch the meat tenderizer.

It's a good idea to include a small container of meat tenderizer in your family first aid box. Pain will stop when tenderizer, an enzyme that digests protein, is rubbed on a bee sting. Speed is important. It won't work if the venom has already spread. Another "remedy" that seems to work well is a slice of onion.

"HIC" CUPS

WHY? Have you ever wondered why you hiccup? When you hiccup, your diaphragm jerks, pulling air into the lungs. If the epiglottis is closed, the air smacks into it so quickly that there's a body jolt. This moves the vocal cords and a "hic" sound comes out.

Try this experiment with your preschooler(s). When the hiccups are no longer welcome, eat a teaspoon of granulated sugar. The hiccups will stop as soon as the sugar is in your mouth.... usually works faster than the water-gulp or scare-boo techniques.

SAFETY

- health inspectors
- firefighters
- paramedics
- police officers
- traffic directors
- gas and electrical inspectors
- inventors of childproof containers
- other

SAFETY AWARENESS

We should all be responsible for safety awareness. Talk with your child(ren) about all the people outside the home who are employed to prevent accidents from happening.

Talk about the importance of their jobs.

Then talk about what we can all do to promote safety in our homes and in our schools. Spend time going over rules for SAFE FUN, in the water, on tricycles or bicycles. Talk about the dangers of electric outlets and plugs, slippery floors from spilled liquid and the dangers of eating outdoor plants, household cleansers and medicines.

You may have to use some demonstrations. If there's a fire on the news, talk about how it started. Pick up a crushed item in the street and personalize street accident awareness. When your child(ren) accidently gets a foot cut from a piece of glass, talk about it right then.

Also, talk about emergency situations. What can a preschooler do if....

- baby brother eats some cleanser or a toadstool?
- you find fire in the house?
- a friend falls off the swing and can't move?
- a stranger offers candy?
- baby sister puts a raisin up her nose?

ACCIDENT PREVENTION

Enjoy the simplicity and relaxed atmosphere of a childproof home. Preschoolers are capable of respecting <u>one</u> valuable per room.... two is pushing it.... and three, FORGET IT!

At the earliest ages, children enjoy pretending they are traffic directors, fire detectives, poison spotters, etc. A make-believe SAFETY HOUSE INSPECTOR, outfitted with an official "inspector's" hat and bag for dangerous items (chokables, eatables, cuttables, etc.), can look for loose rugs, sharp or pointed objects, open medicine cabinets, potentially dangerous matches, etc.

With your child(ren), inspect from room to room:

- garage..... check paint and paint-related products, tools in proper place
- bathroom...... check the razor, medicines, hot water (turn thermostadt to medium if possible), etc.
- kitchen....... handles turned in, hottest pans in back, simmer front .... sharp knives put away....... vitamins, pills, cleansers, etc. locked out of reach.

RED LIGHT, GREEN LIGHT

This game reinforces "traffic safety sense" and is a super energy-releaser. Cut out one large red and one large green construction paper circle. Attach to a stick, "lollipop" fashion. Preschooler(s) lines up at one end of the room, you at the other, holding "lights." Raise the green light....move forward / raise the red..... stop. When s/he reaches you, it's now her/his turn to be Director of Traffic.

NUTRITION

A nutritious diet not only keeps a family healthy, but affects family members' dispositions as well. It is important that children understand the reasons for eating nutritious foods and the negative aspects of the "junks." A well nourished young child has little craving for candy.

(noisy stomach growling)

Grouchy   cranky   ornery

DISCUSS
who helps people stay healthy _outside_ the home..........
...health education experts
...nutritionists
...dietitians
...scientists
...health nurse
in the home?

...WHAT...."JOBS"....DO FOODS DO FOR US?

BUILDING BLOCKS for body repair and growth are proteins. They are usually from animal sources.

FUEL FOODS are carbohydrates. They are starch and sugar foods.

ENERGY PRODUCTION is done by fats. They are the oily foods like butter, margarine, oil, cream, etc.

WHAT DO WE NEED EACH DAY?

- three servings of milk or cheese
- four servings of fruit and vegetables
- four servings of bread and cereals
- two servings of meat or fish

Talk with your preschooler(s) about a food item when he/she is eating it. Children like to know what is happening to their bodies. FOR EXAMPLE, milk has calcium. It helps bones and teeth grow stronger. Then, demonstrate the importance of calcium. Put a small chicken bone in vinegar. The calcium from the bone dissolves leaving only the elastic connective tissues. The bone becomes soft and bends.

NUTRITION WEEK

Plan a nutrition week with your preschooler(s). Let each day represent a food group.

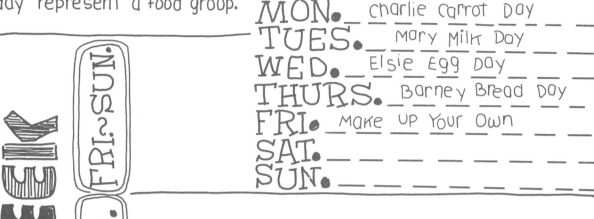

MON. _ Charlie Carrot Day _ _
TUES. _ Mary Milk Day _ _
WED. _ Elsie Egg Day _ _ _
THURS. _ Barney Bread Day _
FRI. _ Make Up Your Own _ _
SAT. _ _ _ _ _ _ _
SUN. _ _ _ _ _ _ _

FRI.~SUN.

THURS.

- visit a bakery
- punch some yeast bread
- make pasta jewelry (sewing: Housekeeping)
- have a make-your-own sandwich party
- make a family sandwich. See page 145.

WED.

- see....eggstra- activities (Meal Preparation)
- learn to crack an egg
- make egg carton animals
- start an egg collection.... include bird, quail, turkey, chicken, etc. (Do not boil)

TUES.

- make butter: you'll need heavy cream in a jar and STRONG MUSCLES. Shake and shake until butter separates and floats to the top.
- think about MILK. If you lived in Lapland you might enjoy yogurt made from reindeer's milk; in Armenia made from buffalo's or goat's milk.
- write your local dairy council for literature.

MON.

- plant a vegetable garden.
- Talk about Charlie's fruit and vegetable relatives... their tastes, textures and colors.
- read I Like Vegetables by Sharon Lerner.
- enjoy a vegetable dip.
- finish lunch with "mother nature's toothbrush" .....the apple.

SOME OTHER TIDBITS

How many peanut butter sandwiches does the average preschooler devour between the terrible twos and kindergarten?

Are you ready to hear about the ever popular peanut butter and honey sandwich?

It isn't easy being a male bee! For every pound of honey he has to make between 40,000 and 80,000 trips, with each trip being as long as 1½ miles (LOVE AT FIRST BITE by J. Cooper)

Let the "busy bee" in your family make HOMEMADE PEANUT BUTTER. Shell 2 cups roasted peanuts. Take off the skins too. Smash some peanuts with a block to show that peanut butter is smashed peanuts. Put the rest through a food grinder or blender. Add 2 tbs. peanut oil and salt to taste.

SOUND FROM INSIDE

Ever wonder about "FANNY BUBBLES" or just plain "gas?" What are those funny little sounds that send preschoolers giggling? One of the by-products of food broken down in one's intestines by bacteria is methane gas. (Yep, the same stuff that powers the kitchen stove!) As food piles up, bacteria multiply, and the result is GAS. Some infamous "gas makers" are beans, cabbage, and Brussels sprouts.

And what about "STOMACH GROWLS?" When your stomach is empty for a long time -- like for 8 hours -- it is mostly filled with gas. Contractions squeeze the gas against the stomach walls causing pants, gurgles and growls. If you have a stethescope..... listen in!

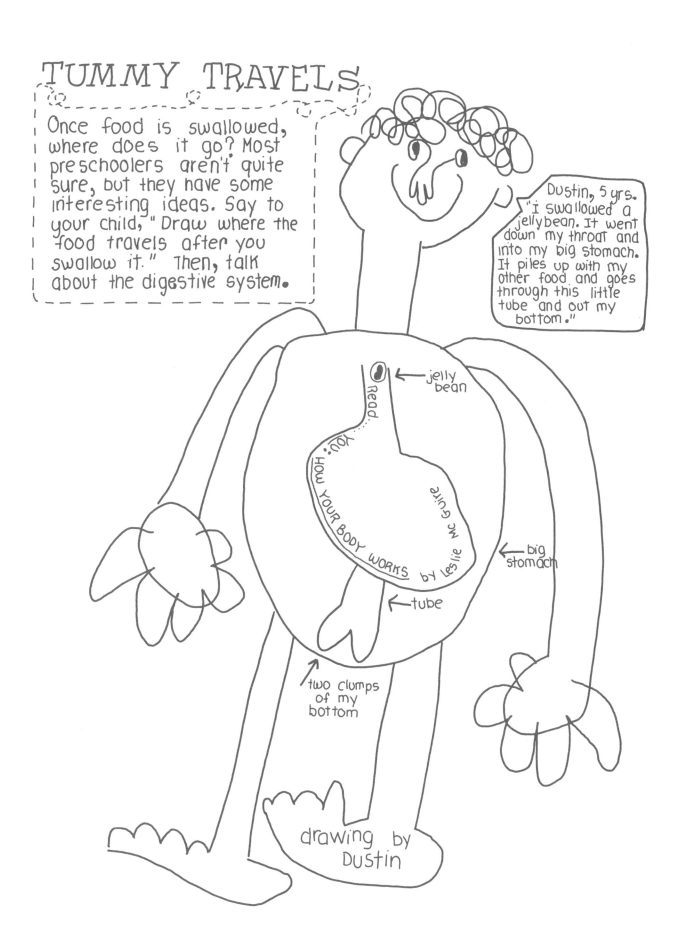

TUMMY TRAVELS

Once food is swallowed, where does it go? Most preschoolers aren't quite sure, but they have some interesting ideas. Say to your child, "Draw where the food travels after you swallow it." Then, talk about the digestive system.

Dustin, 5 yrs. "I swallowed a jellybean. It went down my throat and into my big stomach. It piles up with my other food and goes through this little tube and out my bottom."

jelly bean

Read you: HOW YOUR BODY WORKS by Leslie McGuire

big stomach

tube

two clumps of my bottom

drawing by Dustin

CHILD CARE

- baby dolls
- bathing
- diapering
- singing
- nurturing activities
- the sitter
- books

the kid

Girls are usually encouraged to develop emotionally....to be compassionate, caring, and to take care of others. Training starts young. Boys are often deprived of these experiences and consequently of learning childcare skills.

It is the purpose of this section to present men/women and boys/girls in nurturing roles with activities to practice childcare skills so that children will understand that parenting is a.....................

SHARED RESPONSIBILITY

Five little peewees up in our tree.
Father, mother and babies three.
Father brought a worm.
Mother brought a bug.
Then the three baby peewees all began to tug.
This one ate the bug.
This one ate the worm.
This one said, "The next will be my turn."

Father........thumb
Mother........first finger
Babies........other fingers
Touch the right finger as the
    family member is mentioned.

Things to discuss.....
with your child(ren):

● who takes care of babies?
● who took care of you when you
    were a baby?
● what did they do?
● why do babies cry?
● what are some ways you could
    help a baby?
● what could you teach a baby?
● talk about when your
    preschooler was a baby
    .... first words, favorite
    game, etc.
● look through his/her
    baby album.

CHILD CARE

Preschoolers begin early to form their nurturing interests. The baby doll takes center stage.

The baby doll used in dramatic play is often the center of practicing nurturing skills. Preschoolers seem to establish two specific relationships with dolls...... one THE COMPANION DOLL, the other THE BABY DOLL, which a child recognizes as a weaker personality, dependent,...... a figure that needs to be protected and provided for.

Preschoolers are imitating their parents' behavior (feeding, dressing, talking to, etc.) and at the same time developing those emotional sets of responses that lead to loving and caring. A child is learning that he/she will be needed by others.

When your child asks for a doll, select **one as lifelike as available**. Who wants to cuddle up to a stiff piece of vinyl? Points to consider: life-size, open and close eyes, soft skin, newborn arms and legs, and appropriate sex.

Preschoolers will teach you alot about your own nurturing skills; they are mirrors.

BABY DOLLS

SEE the doll section in the INFLUENCES CHAPTER!

- Baby Tender Love and Baby Brother Tender Love.... white and black versions, physically correct (M)
- Sasha Dolls... ethnic dolls (CP)
- Joey Stivic (Ideal) the anatomically accurate grandson of Archie Bunker.
  - Brother and Sister Dolls (CC)...anatomically correct.

172

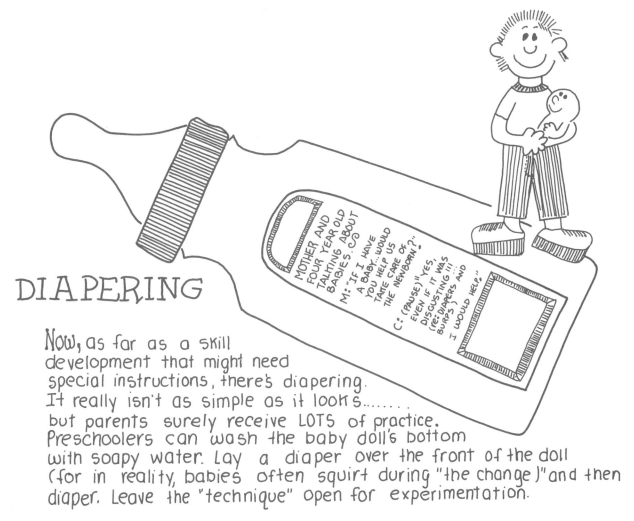

MOTHER AND
FOUR YEAR OLD
TALKING ABOUT
BABIES. ☺☺
M: "IF I HAVE
A BABY...WOULD
YOU HELP US
TAKE CARE OF
THE NEWBORN?"

C: (PAUSE)"YES,
EVEN IF IT WAS
DISGUSTING !!!
(re: DIAPERS AND
BURPS.)
I WOULD HELP."

DIAPERING

Now, as far as a skill
development that might need
special instructions, there's diapering.
It really isn't as simple as it looks........
but parents surely receive LOTS of practice.
Preschoolers can wash the baby doll's bottom
with soapy water. Lay a diaper over the front of the doll
(for in reality, babies often squirt during "the change)" and then
diaper. Leave the "technique" open for experimentation.

BATHING

Then, there's bathing. Children love to bathe their baby dolls;
babies love baths. Provide lots of space in an area you
don't mind getting wet..... include tearless shampoo, sponge
and towel.

SINGING

Singing is a favorite nurturing activity of children. Lullabyes
often provide that needed "quiet time." The scene is a rocking
chair, baby doll, bottle and song. A few old standbys are:

- Twinkle, twinkle little star
- Are you sleeping? Brother John, Sister Jane
- Rock-a-bye baby
- Where is Thumbkin?
- Eensy, weensy spider

NURTURING ACTIVITIES

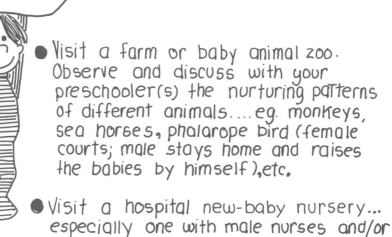

- Visit a farm or baby animal zoo. Observe and discuss with your preschooler(s) the nurturing patterns of different animals....eg. monkeys, sea horses, phalarope bird (female courts; male stays home and raises the babies by himself),etc.

- Visit a hospital new-baby nursery... especially one with male nurses and/or where both parents share a hospital room.

- Visit a friend with a baby.... encourage a preschool boy as well as a girl to hold, love and feed the newborn.

MENTAL HEALTH BREAK

Do you have the afternoon droops? Sleepy?

According to researchers Drs. John M. Taub, Peter E. Tanuay and Douglas Clarkson, persons who nap consistently are.... MORE ALERT, LESS TENSE and in general IN A BETTER MOOD!

So take twenty or sixty if you can. Sweet dreams.

RESOURCES

DIAPERING: scrap material and safety pins for older preschoolers; paper towels and mini band aids for disposables, cornstarch or petroleum jelly if you're daring, changing blanket BATH: large bowl, toweling, cotton balls, OTHER: baby bottles, rocking chair, stroller, toys, baby clothes, eating ware, etc.

MY FAMILY PLAY PEOPLE (MB)
Black and white family groups....2 parent age people, 2 older people, 1 teenager, 1 child. The females do not wear aprons or have babies painted in their arms. The stand-up forms are drawn with great detail and are complete, front and back.

MEN IN NURTURING ROLE (W.A.A.)
Eight black and white photographs of men caring for young children. 8" x 10". There are fathers, grandfathers, and men who work with young children... eg. teachers

THIS IS MY FATHER AND ME (LM)...30 B+W photographs of fathers with children from many countries.

THE SITTER

Being very careful in selecting baby sitters is vitally important, for they are "parent substitutes" and have a tremendous influence upon preschoolers. For successful non-sexist sitter selection, consider the following pointers:

- Alternate between male and female sitters.
- Talk to your sitter about sex role stereotypes.
- Explain the sharing, helping, non-sexist environment you are creating.... include role modeling, sexist language, influences, etc.
- Ask your sitter to read LIBERATING YOUNG CHILDREN FROM SEX ROLES by Phyllis Taube Greenleaf, New England Free Press. The book has twenty-two consciousness-raising pages. OR BABY-SITTING: A CONCISE GUIDE (LM) Practical information for boys and girls.

WILLIAM'S DOLL   by Charlotte Zolotow
    Father says no when William wants a doll, but
    Grandmother understands a doll will help William
    become a better father.

DADDY LONG EARS   by Robert Kraus
    Daddy Long Ears is "left" to raise thirty-one bunny
    rabbits, which includes washing, cooking and other
    childcare responsibilities.

THE DADDY BOOK   by Robert Stewart
    Fathers are shown in traditional and non-traditional
    roles. They are pictured in several childcare jobs,
    such as changing diapers, cooking for children, playing,
    helping at bathtime, etc.

GO AND HUSH THE BABY   by Betsy Byars
    Big brother finds out that babysitting can be fun.
    He entertains his baby brother with songs, magic
    tricks and stories.

ON MOTHER'S LAP   by Ann Herbert Scott
    Michael, an Eskimo boy, snuggles on his mother's
    lap with his blanket, boat and doll.

CHILDREN AND THEIR FATHERS edited by Hanns Reich Verlag
    Photos of fathers and children.   Multi cultural.

ZEEK SILVER MOON   by Amy Ehrlich
    An exquisitely illustrated book showing the spon-
    taneous affection and humor between child
    and father. Zeek's father makes him a
    cradle and sings him a lullaby he made up.

MARTIN'S FATHER   by Margrit Eichler (LP)
    Martin spends the day with his dad
    doing the laundry, making sandwiches, etc.

JUST THINK by Betty Miles and Joan Blos
    Shows mothers who work outside
    the home and fathers enjoying
    their children.

raising Parents isn't easy

FATHER POWER by Henry Biller and Dennis Meredith
   A useful guide in helping men to become active and
   equal participants with women in childrearing. However,
   the authors frequently make use of sex stereotyping.

NON-SEXIST CHILD RAISING by Carrie Carmichael
   An interesting account of what a wide variety of
   American families have experienced in endeavoring to
   bring up their children free of gender prejudice.

FATHER FEELINGS   by Eliot A. Daley
   A straightforward and personal account of one year
   with the author's family. Feelings are expressed throughout and changing sex role expectations examined.

HOW TO RAISE INDEPENDENT AND PROFESSIONALLY SUCCESSFUL
   DAUGHTERS by Dr. Rita and Dr. Kenneth Dunn
   A comprehensive guide that includes facts and suggestions. Chapter 3, "What to Do from Age Two to Five" is
   especially pertinent for preschool parents.

LIBERATED PARENTS - LIBERATED CHILDREN by Faber and Mazlish
   Practical ideas on childrearing.

RIGHT FROM THE START: A GUIDE TO NON-SEXIST CHILD REARING
        by Selma Greenberg. This enlightening book examines
   the ways which children are limited by traditional methods
   of child rearing and offers practical alternatives.

WHO WILL RAISE THE CHILDREN? NEW OPTIONS FOR FATHERS
   (AND MOTHERS) by James A. Levine
   Fathers' traditional involvement in childrearing is evaluated.
   Examples are cited of different ways in which fathers
   are becoming more involved.

TENDERNESS IS STRENGTH: FROM MACHISMO TO MANHOOD
   by Harold C. Lyons, Jr. Addressed to men, this book
   discusses how men can be tender in all relationships,
   including those with children.

PARENTS' YELLOW PAGES by the Princeton Center for Infancy
   A directory of services, products and useful
   information for parents.

(Continued on next page)

WE CAN CHANGE IT by Susan Shargel and Irene Kane
   (Change for Children), 2588 Mission St., San Francisco, CA 94110)
   A pamphlet that suggests non-sexist books and ways for
   adults to help in countering sex-role stereotyping.
FATHER JOURNAL   by David Steinberg
   A personal account of a young father's growing realization of
   his nurturing feelings toward his six-year-old son which he
   credits to his wife's involvement with feminist groups.

more RESOURCES ILLUSTRATING
NON-TRADITIONAL ROLE MODELS

CHILDREN'S NON-SEXIST COLORING BOOK (RI)
   People young and old are shown in non-traditional roles
WHAT PARENTS DO   by Jan Harper (WP)
   Parents are pictured in non-traditional careers and doing
   things together, such as being farmers, running a business,
   and building boats.
ARTHUR AND CLEMENTINE by Adela Turin and Nella Bosnia (WRPC)
   Clementine the Turtle rejects being burdened with carrying a
   "skyscraper" of materialistic household items on her back
   and leaves to find her own way in the world.
THE BREADTIME STORY by Adela Turin and Margherita Saccaro (WRPC)
   Inga, a young girl, liberates a town of little women who just
   prepare sandwiches for the BIG men who work in the BIG BUILD-
   ING. In the end, men and women become the same relative size
   and help each other.
THE SUMMER NIGHT by Charlotte Zolotow
   A special relationship is shown between a little girl and her dad.
A FAMILY OF POTTERS   by Jan Harper (WP)
   A young girl helps her father solve a problem and saves the
   pots her mother makes.
ALL KINDS OF MOTHERS   by Cecily Brownstone
THE FORTUNATE CATASTROPHE by Turin and Bosnia (WRPC)* p.141.
MARTIN'S FATHER   by M. Eichler (LP) * p.141
FRESH FISH... AND CHIPS by Andrews (CWEP) * p.202
GROWNUPS CRY, TOO   by Nancy Hazen (L.P)
   Adults as well as children cry for many different reasons
THE DADDY BOOK by Stewart * p.176
"PARENTS" a poster by Dale (WMCLC) * p.187

* See this page for the annotated bibliography.

 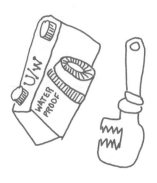

Have you ever watched a child's face light up while talking with a firefighter, circus clown, or deep-sea diver?

OR, noticed the intensity of concentration exhibited by a youngster observing a baker, plumber, or veterinarian caring for the child's pet?

OR seen children mesmerized by a champion skater, dancer, or ball player? In other words, the world of work is fascinating to young children!

? Why? The purpose of this chapter is to expose children to a variety of careers and to present work as more equally shared by males and females. We want children to know that there are a great many career choices open to them and that no one career is only for males or only for females.

CHAPTER 6

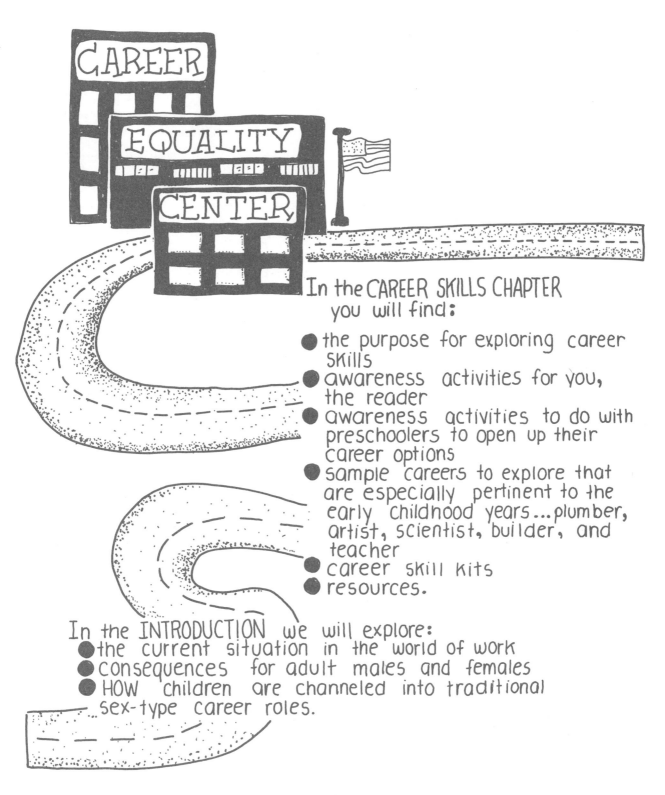

In the CAREER SKILLS CHAPTER
you will find:

- the purpose for exploring career skills
- awareness activities for you, the reader
- awareness activities to do with preschoolers to open up their career options
- sample careers to explore that are especially pertinent to the early childhood years...plumber, artist, scientist, builder, and teacher
- career skill kits
- resources.

In the INTRODUCTION we will explore:
- the current situation in the world of work
- consequences for adult males and females
- HOW children are channeled into traditional sex-type career roles.

Too often <u>hiring</u> and <u>promotion</u> are based on sex rather than on abilities and interests. And, too often, the potential for these are not developed because of tradition dictating that certain skills and interests should be developed related to one's sex ONLY.

Much of the current division of labor has been based on tradition and history. But do these reflect today's realities? We all know women who DO use their brains and/or DO labor..... and men who are gentle, nurturant, and/or artistic.

Even when women have been able to gain entry into male-dominated fields, usually they are stuck at the lower-status positions; they are not promoted as often or as quickly into the higher-level, decision making positions. This even holds true in female-dominated fields; for example, in education, only 20% of the elementary principals are female.

Quite a discrepancy also exists in terms of <u>earnings</u>. In the U.S. women's average earnings as compared to those of men's in similar jobs have <u>decreased</u> year by year. In 1957 65% of what men earned was earned by women... in 1976 it was <u>56%</u>! (U.S. Dept. of Labor.)

The average women in 1974 earned only $3.00 for every $5.00 paid to a man in a similar job! (Chavetz, 1974)

And get this! In 1974 a high school male graduate...... averaged $12,000 a year while a female <u>college</u>.... graduate averaged only $9,000 a year! (Guttentag and Bray, 1976)

SHOULD THESE DISCREPANCIES EXIST?

Many people maintain that these are O.k..... men should earn more as they are the providers for their families and women work only for "pin money." Also, many women have never developed career skills because they have thought of motherhood as a life-long career. Yet, what about women who:

- are divorced or single and support themselves?
- are heads of households and support children?
- are highly intelligent and/or have highly developed skills?

Should they make less for the same work or be kept at lower level positions JUST BECAUSE they are women? And what happens to women...

- when their children go off to school?
- when/if their marriages end up in divorce?
- when/if necessity dictates that they get a job?

IT'S A FACT

Among all poor families, more than 2 out of 5 are headed by women. Almost 2 out of 3 poor black families are headed by women.

As of 1974:
43% of all married women were working
46% of all women with children under 18 were working
63% of all working mothers had children between 6-17 years
19% of all working mothers had children under 3 years
(U.S. Dept. of Labor, 1975).

The average age for a woman to have her last child is 26 years old.

She is then in her mid-thirties when her last child is in school most of the day.

WHAT DOES SHE DO THEN?

So many women do work. 43% of the labor force today is composed of women. And, the U.S. Department of Labor projects that 9 out of 10 girls will work in their adult lives.

"It is the mind, not the body, that society needs now, and woman's mind is equal to man's." (Freeman, 1973)

If so many girls are probably going to be working at some time in their lives, why not START preparing them now to be receptive to a variety of occupations and professions? Preschoolers are learning alot now about jobs and most of what they are learning is sex-stereotyped.

A group of first and second graders, when asked, "what would you like to be when you grow up," listed 18 occupations if they were boys, as compared to 8 if they were girls...which were all sex-typed. (Looft, 1971)

WHAT IS HE DISCOURAGED FROM DOING?

With regards to boys, we find that they too are channeled and limited, although as men they have had many more jobs open to them as well as being paid more.

However, they are very much discouraged from entering "women's fields," such as nursing, teaching, dancing, etc. This is UNFAIR to them as well as to people who could be benefiting from their participation.

And, men suffer more so than do women from health problems and are not usually given the option of working or staying at home. Traditionally, women have had much more of a choice.

Preschool children are exposed to many influences.. role models, toys, television, books, and school. ...WHAT YOU CAN DO is to provide some alternatives which hopefully will have some impact on the force of all the other influences. It is not that we want girls to assume the traditional male role with regard to what they will be doing as future adults or vice versa for boys. Rather, we can OPEN things up so that neither will be so channeled and consequently so limited. The activities presented in the remainder of this chapter are ways you can do this.

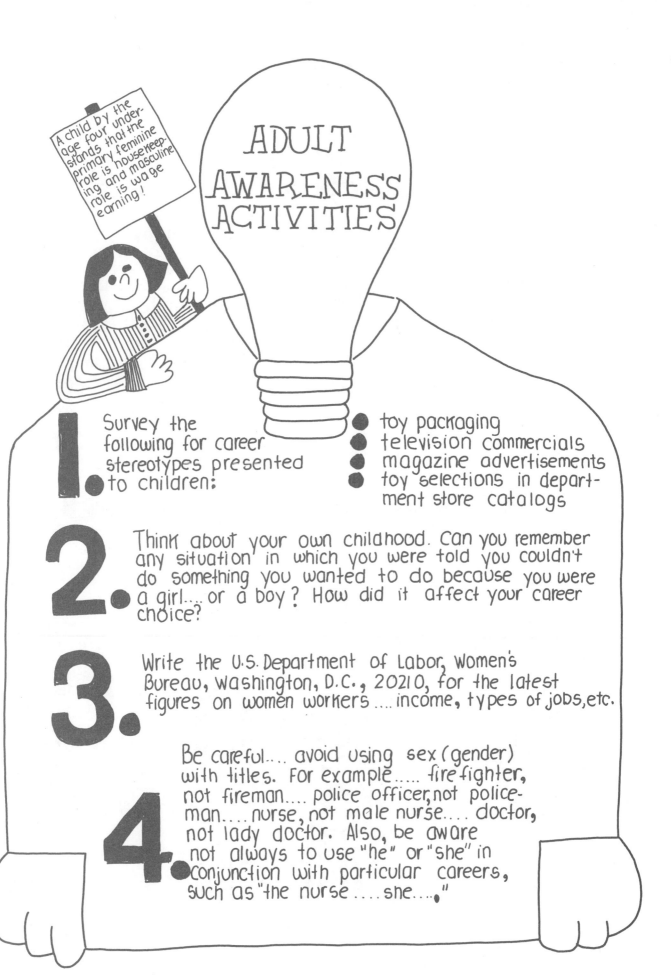

A child by the age four understands that the primary feminine role is housekeeping and masculine role is wage earning!

ADULT AWARENESS ACTIVITIES

1. Survey the following for career stereotypes presented to children:

- toy packaging
- television commercials
- magazine advertisements
- toy selections in department store catalogs

2. Think about your own childhood. Can you remember any situation in which you were told you couldn't do something you wanted to do because you were a girl.... or a boy? How did it affect your career choice?

3. Write the U.S. Department of Labor, Women's Bureau, Washington, D.C., 20210, for the latest figures on women workers ....income, types of jobs, etc.

4. Be careful.... avoid using sex (gender) with titles. For example..... fire fighter, not fireman.... police officer, not policeman.... nurse, not male nurse.... doctor, not lady doctor. Also, be aware not always to use "he" or "she" in conjunction with particular careers, such as "the nurse ....she....."

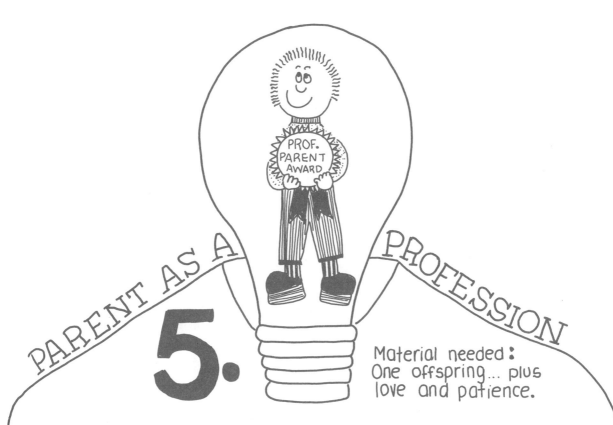

PARENT AS A PROFESSION

5.

Material needed:
One offspring... plus love and patience.

Parents, think of all that you do in your parent role. With what kinds of careers are you involved? Did you realize that you may be all of these : artist, baker, barber, beautician, bookkeeper, buyer, cook, counselor, dietician, mechanic, gardener, janitor, painter, photographer, practical nurse, recreation specialist, sanitarian, seamstress/mender, veterinarian, waiter/ waitress, windowwasher, chauffeur, repair person, and teacher? What does this say for your worth and your skills? (It would make quite an impressive resume.)

Most young preschoolers want to help parents do things around the home, e.g. pulling weeds, cooking, etc. Take advantage of their present enthusiasm (which may dissipate later) by having them explore parental roles.

Read A TERRIBLE THING THAT HAPPENED AT OUR HOUSE by Marge Blaine A wonderfully written and illustrated book about the turmoil and eventual resolution in a family when the mother returns to work as a science teacher and the father and children gradually learn what it takes to keep a family functioning.

Parents by Rae Dale, a poster of parents in 12 different non-traditional roles. (WMCLC)

* Check role models (page 178) for other resources.

CHILDREN AWARENESS

CENTER

1. <u>EXPOSE</u> child (ren) to on-the-job workers, including some in non-traditional careers, such as:
- woman pediatrician and/or dentist
- male nurse/hygenist
- male dancer in a dance performance
- male teachers in a preschool
- female and male waiters, cooks, chefs in a restaurant
- male/female barbers in a hair salon or barber shop.
- male/female construction workers
- others

2. Invent a silly-sounding job title for a specific task you'd like accomplished, for example, maybe a....
- zoo-feeder
- dust-duster
- plant-mister
- pillow-fluffer
- weed-puller
- finger print-magician

Props can add to the reality of your newly created occupation.

Write the new job title on a piece of paper and tape it to the front of an old hat. Send your worker off to explore a new career.

3. <u>READ</u>

<u>I Can Be Anything You Can Be</u> by Joel Rothman Presents boys and girls in matching career choices from conductor to umpire to jockey, etc. Multi-cultural.

4.

<u>MAKE</u> a career opportunity picture book... "Look what I Can Be"
- Collect pictures of people in careers, using traditional sex-limited occupations and non-traditional occupations.... males and females.. all in relatively equal numbers.
- Talk about what these people do.
- If possible include matching pictures of males and females performing the same jobs.
- This book can also be used to help children learn the alphabet. Cut out pictures of careers for each letter of the alphabet, e.g. A-artist, B-barber, etc.
- At the top of each page print a capital and small letter for the appropriate career.
- Adults—read HELP WANTED, a study of sexism in career education materials. (WOMEN ON WORDS AND IMAGES)

6.

<u>INTERVIEW</u> your child(ren) as well as other children about jobs.

- What can girls be?
- What can boys be?
- What they'd like to be when they grow up.

Ask your child(ren) about careers for males and for females. If certain careers are mentioned by sex, ask if the other sex could do that job. If response is negative, ask why. Remember, seeing is believing and FIRST-HAND EXPERIENCE is an effective technique for changing sex role stereotypes

5.

<u>PLAY</u> a career skills card game.
- Argot cards
- Robot cards (F)
- Scarecrow cards (WMCLC)

Non-sexist card games with male and female counterparts in various occupations, played similar to Old Maid.

EXPLORE NOW!

Turn the page and explore some specific careers with your pre-schooler(s).

Plumber

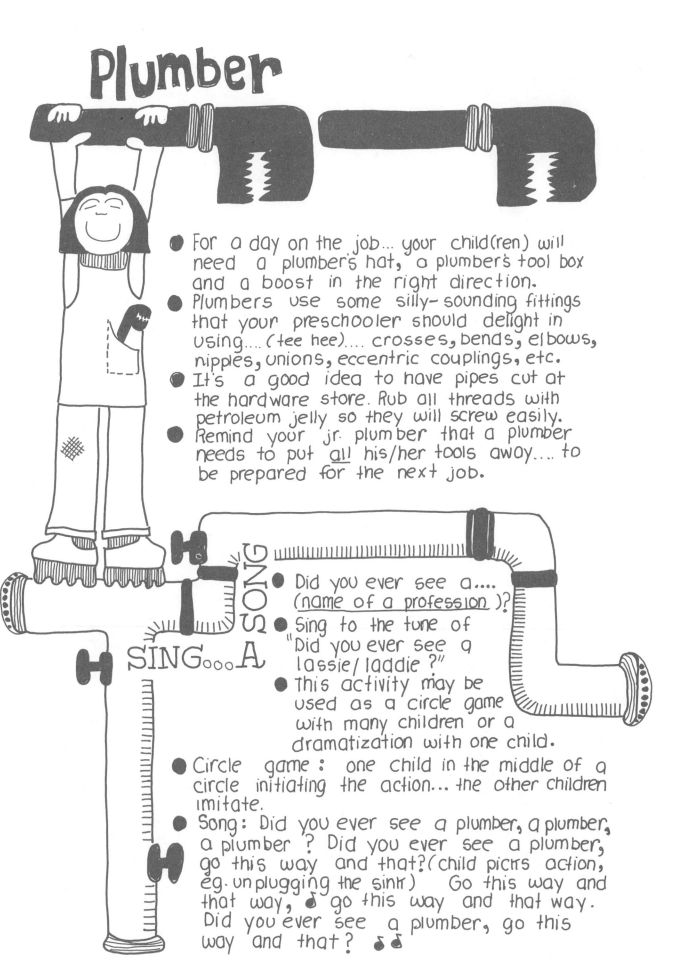

- For a day on the job... your child(ren) will need a plumber's hat, a plumber's tool box and a boost in the right direction.
- Plumbers use some silly-sounding fittings that your preschooler should delight in using.... (tee hee).... crosses, bends, elbows, nipples, unions, eccentric couplings, etc.
- It's a good idea to have pipes cut at the hardware store. Rub all threads with petroleum jelly so they will screw easily.
- Remind your jr. plumber that a plumber needs to put all his/her tools away.... to be prepared for the next job.

SING...A SONG

- Did you ever see a.... (name of a profession)?
- Sing to the tune of "Did you ever see a lassie/laddie ?"
- This activity may be used as a circle game with many children or a dramatization with one child.
- Circle game: one child in the middle of a circle initiating the action... the other children imitate.
- Song: Did you ever see a plumber, a plumber, a plumber? Did you ever see a plumber, go this way and that?(child picks action, e.g. unplugging the sink)   Go this way and that way, ♪ go this way and that way. Did you ever see a plumber, go this way and that? ♪♪

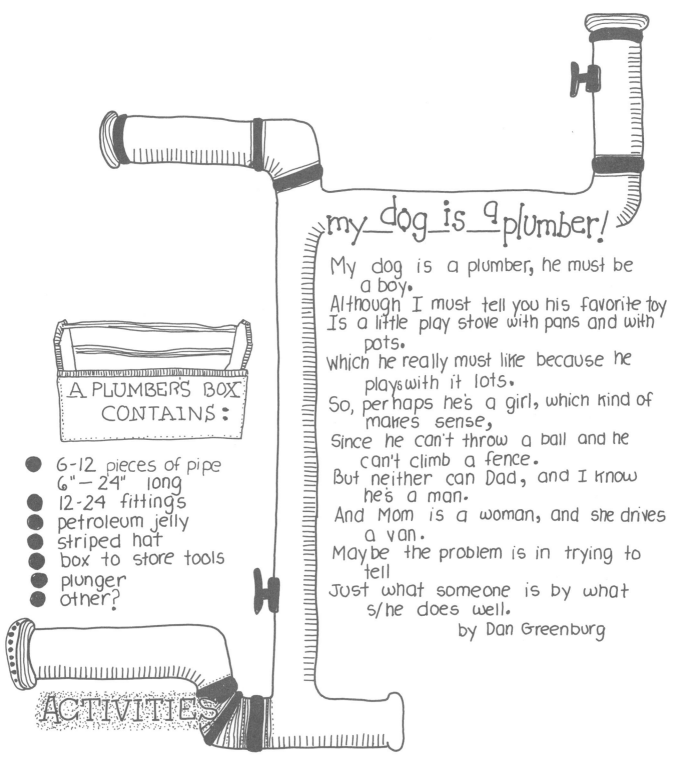

my dog is a plumber!

My dog is a plumber, he must be
    a boy.
Although I must tell you his favorite toy
Is a little play stove with pans and with
    pots.
Which he really must like because he
    plays with it lots.
So, perhaps he's a girl, which kind of
    makes sense,
Since he can't throw a ball and he
    can't climb a fence.
But neither can Dad, and I know
    he's a man.
And Mom is a woman, and she drives
    a van.
Maybe the problem is in trying to
    tell
Just what someone is by what
    s/he does well.
                    by Dan Greenburg

A PLUMBER'S BOX CONTAINS:

- 6-12 pieces of pipe
  6" — 24" long
- 12-24 fittings
- petroleum jelly
- striped hat
- box to store tools
- plunger
- other?

ACTIVITIES

- Unplug a stopped-up sink together
- Tighten a leaky faucet together
- Start a collection: different sizes
    and kinds of fittings, etc.

SCIENTIST

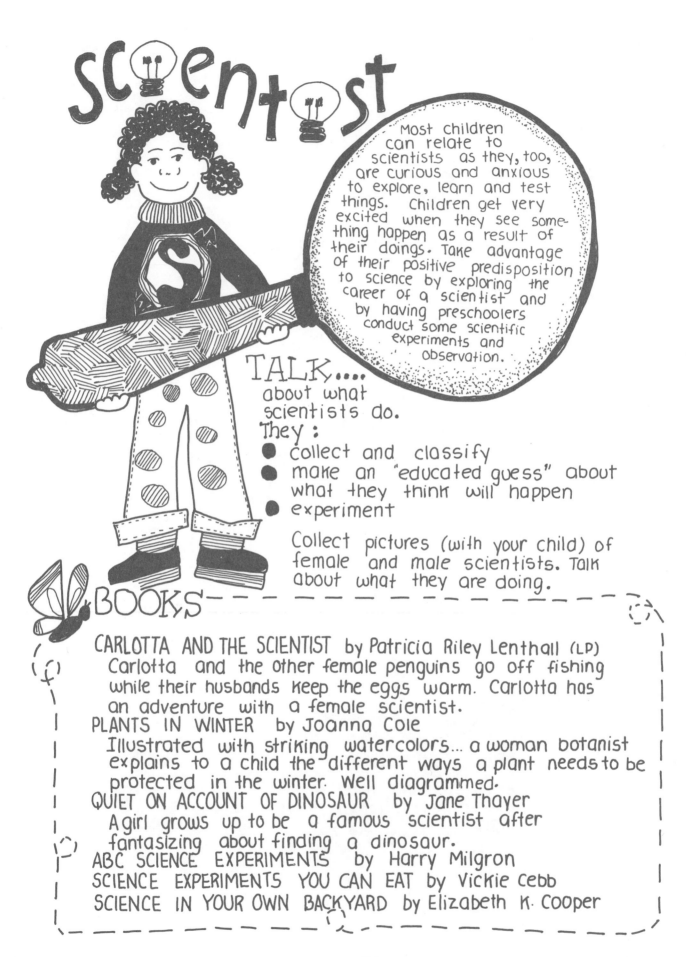

Most children can relate to scientists as they, too, are curious and anxious to explore, learn and test things. Children get very excited when they see something happen as a result of their doings. Take advantage of their positive predisposition to science by exploring the career of a scientist and by having preschoolers conduct some scientific experiments and observation.

TALK....
about what scientists do. They:
- collect and classify
- make an "educated guess" about what they think will happen
- experiment

Collect pictures (with your child) of female and male scientists. Talk about what they are doing.

BOOKS

CARLOTTA AND THE SCIENTIST by Patricia Riley Lenthall (LP)
Carlotta and the other female penguins go off fishing while their husbands keep the eggs warm. Carlotta has an adventure with a female scientist.

PLANTS IN WINTER by Joanna Cole
Illustrated with striking watercolors... a woman botanist explains to a child the different ways a plant needs to be protected in the winter. Well diagrammed.

QUIET ON ACCOUNT OF DINOSAUR by Jane Thayer
A girl grows up to be a famous scientist after fantasizing about finding a dinosaur.

ABC SCIENCE EXPERIMENTS by Harry Milgron

SCIENCE EXPERIMENTS YOU CAN EAT by Vickie Cebb

SCIENCE IN YOUR OWN BACKYARD by Elizabeth K. Cooper

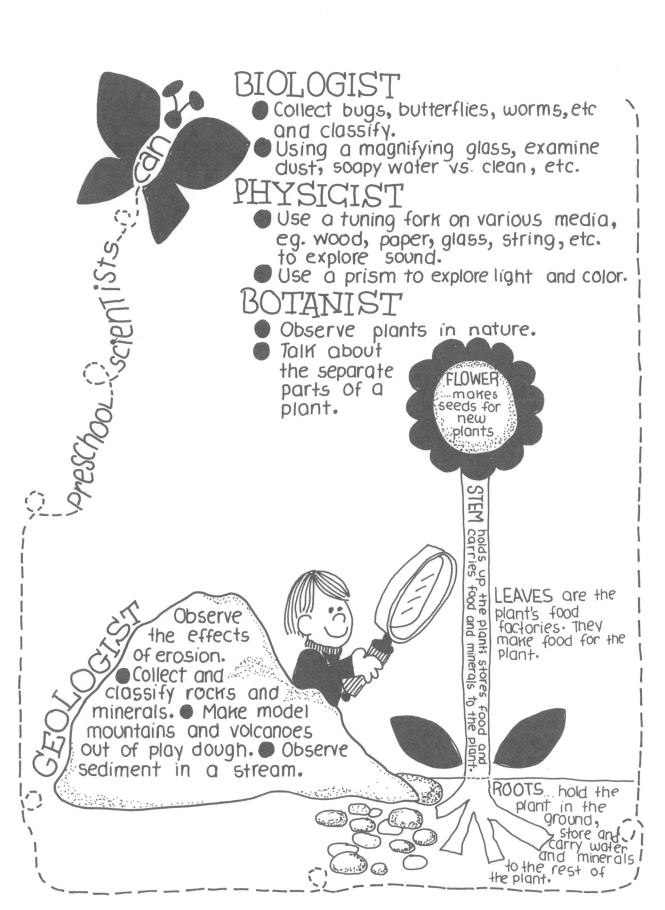

BIOLOGIST
- Collect bugs, butterflies, worms, etc and classify.
- Using a magnifying glass, examine dust, soapy water vs. clean, etc.

PHYSICIST
- Use a tuning fork on various media, eg. wood, paper, glass, string, etc. to explore sound.
- Use a prism to explore light and color.

BOTANIST
- Observe plants in nature.
- Talk about the separate parts of a plant.

preschool scientists... can

FLOWER...makes seeds for new plants

STEM holds up the plant; carries food and minerals to the plant; stores food and

LEAVES are the plant's food factories. They make food for the plant.

GEOLOGIST
Observe the effects of erosion. ● Collect and classify rocks and minerals. ● Make model mountains and volcanoes out of play dough. ● Observe sediment in a stream.

ROOTS... hold the plant in the ground, store and carry water and minerals to the rest of the plant.

193

Teacher

As preschoolers are themselves continuously learning as well as wanting to become independent and to achieve, they seem to be fascinated with teachers and with wanting to <u>teach others</u>. By a child doing the teaching, she/he can feel capable as well as learn by doing. Provide opportunities for your child- (ren) to role-play a teacher... with you, stuffed animals, dolls or other children as students.

talk about:

Start now to help preschoolers develop their awareness skills.... being observant of non-sexist class room environments. Note.....
- who gets to do what?
- the play/work clothes
- use of blocks/carpentry/ "family" house
- activities boys do/ girls do... why?

ACTIVITIES

with your help, your..... preschool teacher can read to "..students" (non-sexist picture books) and/or plan and lead a child care center activity. Start with something simple like play dough. Others:
- storytime
- snack time
- easel painting
- sand play
- outdoor play
- music time
- blocks
- "family" house
- science
- art center

MOTIVATING ACTIVITIES can be used to set into action teacher dramatic play and role modeling.

- Visit a preschool class, preferably non-sexist, multi-cultural, if your child is not already in one. Talk about a teacher's responsibilities. (See Influence Chapter...on The School, pages 64-66.)
- Interview a teacher with your child. Questions? What do you do? What do you like best about teaching?
- If your child is already in a pre-school, possibly the school can arrange child-oriented "teacher-for-a-time" activity. For example; Lead a song or fingerplay in front of the class, greet the arriving students, ring the bell, conduct nap time, etc.
- Read books that are centered around child care centers so that preschoolers will have input into their "memory banks." Suggestions:
  Joshua's Day by Sandra Lucas Surowiecki (LP),
  Will I Have A Friend? by Miriam Cohen,
  Best Friends by Miriam Cohen.
- Watch a T.V. teacher... Mr. Rogers, Captain Kangaroo, etc.
- Initiate dramatic play with a toy school house or school bus (Fisher-Price).
- Read Leo, The Late Bloomer by Robert Kraus. Illustrates the "readiness" principle.

SUPPLIES
- blackboard / flannel board
- school bell
- paper/pencils..."lots"
- picture books
- pointer
- easel/paints
- clay, chalk, crayons, etc
- teacher books eg., Dr. Seus's ABC and ABC Workbook by Jean Mangi (FP)
- and "students"

THE BUILDER

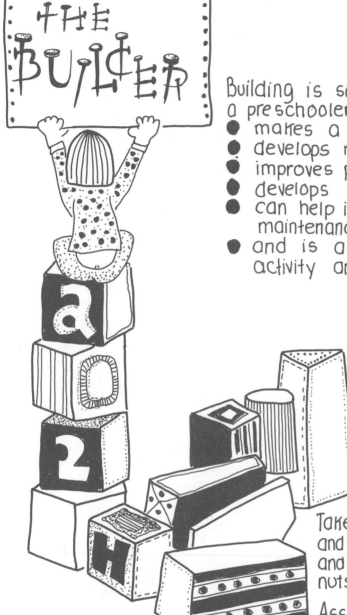

Building is serious business to a preschooler. Building:

- makes a child feel grown up
- develops muscle coordination
- improves problem solving techniques
- develops language skills
- can help in learning and using home maintenance skills
- and is a super-involving-vigorous activity and energy releaser!

GADGET BOARD

To encourage the use of an assortment of tools... make a gadget board.

Take a large wooden board (softwood) and all kinds of hardware.... padlock and key, screen door hook, light switches, nuts, bolts, screws, sliding door bolt, etc.

Assemble. To ensure easy manipulation, rub hardware with bar soap and work the screws until they move easily.

ALPHA BLOCKS CONSTRUCTION SET

40 durable letter blocks, 87 connecting rods. (cc)

GIANT TOYMAKER SET (CC)

... includes girders, wheels, nuts and bolts. 500 pieces

THE CARPENTER

COMBINE one preschooler, a tool box, scrap materials, and a safe work area. MIX .... be prepared to be amazed at the creativity from this unstructured activity.

HAMMERING SURFACES
- cardboard
- styrofoam
- egg cartons
- soft pine

BUILDING MATERIALS
- household discards
- thread spools
- popsicle sticks
- pop tops/corks
- bottle caps
- small boxes

BEGINNING PROJECTS
- fishing pole...(stick, nails, string and magnet)
- boat.....wood, large nail, magnet to pull
- musical nails.... assorted large nails, "thin" strong string, and a board to hang the nails from. Play a tune by hitting the hanging nails with a large nail.

RESOURCES
- take-apart tools, plastic (CG)
- workbench (CG)
- tinker tools, plastic (CG)
- the Toymaker... 80 piece construction set (CC)
- THE TOOL BOX by Anne and Harlow Rockwell

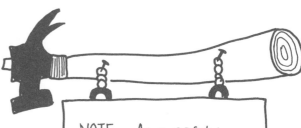

NOTE.... As a safety precaution, preschool carpenters work best ALONE without other children around and with adult supervision.

TOOL BOX

Not all the following tools are necessary. Start off with whatever extra tools are around.
- yardstick
- pencil
- 8-penny nails, large heads
- 10 oz. claw hammer
- brace and bit
- small monkey wrench
- glue
- pliers
- assorted nuts and bolts
- small magnets
- soft wood
- string

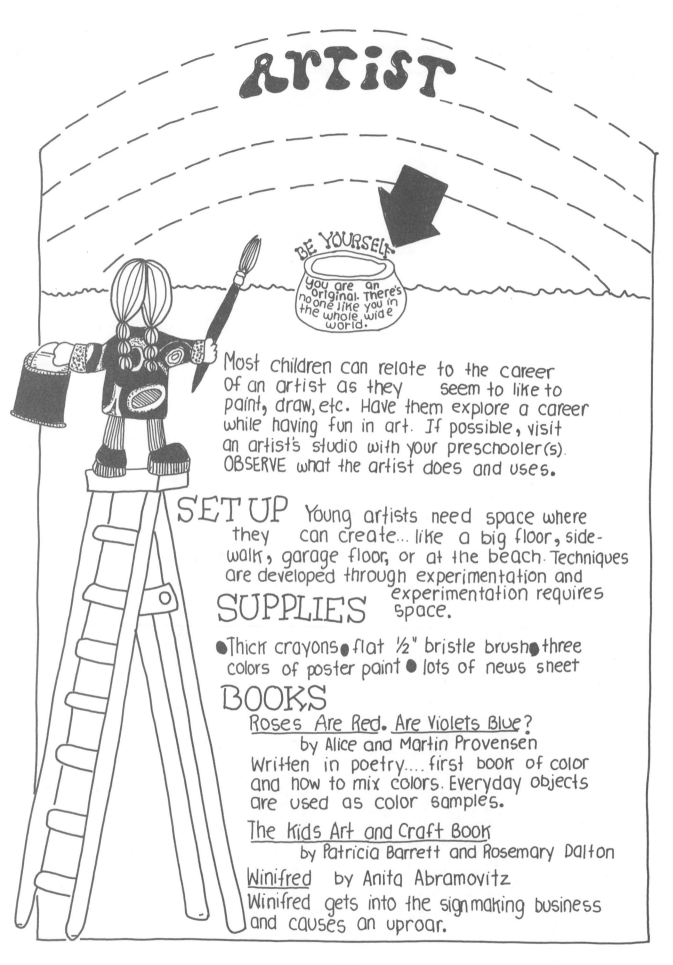

ARTIST

BE YOURSELF You are an original. There's no one like you in the whole wide world.

Most children can relate to the career of an artist as they seem to like to paint, draw, etc. Have them explore a career while having fun in art. If possible, visit an artist's studio with your preschooler(s). OBSERVE what the artist does and uses.

SET UP
Young artists need space where they can create... like a big floor, sidewalk, garage floor, or at the beach. Techniques are developed through experimentation and experimentation requires space.

SUPPLIES

- Thick crayons, flat ½" bristle brush, three colors of poster paint, lots of news sheet

BOOKS

<u>Roses Are Red. Are Violets Blue?</u>
by Alice and Martin Provensen
Written in poetry.... first book of color and how to mix colors. Everyday objects are used as color samples.

<u>The Kids Art and Craft Book</u>
by Patricia Barrett and Rosemary Dalton

<u>Winifred</u> by Anita Abramovitz
Winifred gets into the signmaking business and causes an uproar.

ACTIVITIES

SHAVING CREAM ARTIST
This imaginative artisan can best do his/her creating during bath time. Ingredients.... one preschooler in "birthday" suit, one can of shaving cream, and a painting surface (shower wall, bottom of tub or even a tummy).

The young artist draws pictures in the cream with his/her fingers and hands. Clean up is a few splashes and rinse away. If you decide to move this creative adventure to a drier environment, use newsprint with powder poster paint sprinkled on the shaving cream for an unusual effect.

PUDDING ARTIST
For the "hungrier artist" try instant pudding on butcher paper OR, if you don't want to keep the art work, let your preschooler pudding paint in a T.V. tray. Guaranteed minimal cleanup. Chocolate and butterscotch are big favorites.

SIDEWALK ART SALE
An art sale can help illustrate the more practical side of this career choice. You will need a table, art sale sign, a make-shift cash box and a picnic lunch to tide over your preschool artisan... PLUS an abundance of painted art objects. Painted rocks and/or driftwood are super sellers. Let your preschooler run the sale.

KINDS OF ARTISTS
Are you ready for this. Just a few artistic techniques to experiment with together.... ● paint to music ● finger paint ● brush paint ● body paint ● sponge paint ● string paint ● vegetable printing ● sand and birdseed painting (for a different sensory experience) ● whipped soap ● flakes painting ● colored chalk on wet paper ● and mud painting OR dry food collages ● three dimensional sculptures with playdough, clay, toothpicks, wood, pasta, straws.... the list is delightfully limitless.

HOW TO USE
CAREER SKILL KITS

Play kits are comprised of inexpensive, easy-to-find-in-the-home materials as well as some purchasable toys. Assemble a few kits in large brown boxes and save for a rainy day. Special career skill books are included for often it takes only a story or on-the-job-visit to "spark" a preschooler to explore a career option.

Be sure to ●●●●●●●●

- ● Plan the area for activity....fire fighters function best outdoors.
- ● Consider clean up....your preschool janitor or custodian can help you there.
- ● Think about time allotment.... space travel is time consuming.
- ● Look through GROWING UP EQUAL for accompanying books, toys and other activity ideas.
- ● Follow up... take child(ren) to see someone actually performing in this career.
- ● Try creating your own career skill activities as well as using our suggested resources... the family car can be a space ship, the front yard... a circus arena and junk mail a jr. mail carrier's delight!

ASTRONAUT

JELLY BEANS FOR BREAKFAST
by Miriam Young
Two girls explore the moon

ATHLETE

Assemble a box of miscellaneous sports equipment; include hats and T-shirt.
MOTHER IS A PITCHER by Maxine Kahn
True story about nine women who play baseball. Told in rhyme by a ten-year-old.   (AOS)

BARBER

"Fuzzy Pumper" (K) Barber chair which when cranked causes dolls hair (playdough) to grow; it can be cut with safe plastic barber tools.

CASHIER

Digital Cash Register-battery operated (CC), play money, box for shopping cart, empty food containers, brown paper sacks, wax fruit, Supermarket-reinforced fiberboard, 5 feet tall (CC).

DETECTIVE

Old coat and hat, magnifying glass, and a mystery case to solve, e.g.,"The Case of the Missing Tennis Shoe."

DANCER

Leotards, dance shoes and records.
THE DANCERS by Walter D. Meyer
Michael, a young black boy, meets a ballerina who goes home with him and dances with family and friends.

DOCTOR
NURSE

White shirt, stethoscope, band aids, cotton balls, tongue depressors and a few patients.
Woman doctor doll and male nurse doll-handmade (PP)
MY DOCTOR by Harlow Rockwell
  A boy visits a woman doctor for his checkup.
DRAGON AND THE DOCTOR by Barbara Danish (FP)
  A little girl who is a doctor fixes the tail of a nice dragon.
TOMMY GOES TO THE DOCTOR by Guinilla Wolde
  Tommy goes to a woman doctor for a checkup and is shown the instruments she uses.
MY MOMMY IS A DOCTOR record or cassette,... page 205.
Other resources... pages. 161-163.

201

FARMER
SHEEP BOOK by Carmen Goodyear (LP)
A California farmer shears her sheep, prepares the wool and makes a sweater.
CHARLIE NEEDS A CLOAK by Tomie de Paola
Charlie needs a cloak, so he shows us the step-by-step process from sheep to finished product.
TURNABOUT by William Wiesner
When a farmer and his wife exchange roles for a day, he encounters disasters while she gets along quite well.

FIRE FIGHTER
The garden hose (connected or disconnected due to personal adult preference), fire fighter hat, raincoat and boots.
Female fire fighter doll (PP)
FIRE GIRL by Rich Gibson (FP)

FISH CATCHER
"Let's Go Fishing" Game (CC)
Stick or dowling, yarn, feather for lure, bait and a pond
FISH FOR SUPPER by M.B. Goffstein
Story of a grandmother who fishes every day.
FRESH FISH... AND CHIPS by Jane Andrews (CWEP)
The mother is a "fisher person" in this coloring book. She sets out to catch an assortment of exotic sea creatures.

FLORIST
Blunt-nose scissors, vase, greenery and flowers. Remember to cut flowers in the early morning. Arrange and take flowers to a sick or sad friend. Visit a florist... the colors, smells and textures are guaranteed to lift one's spirits.

HOUSE PAINTER
Painter's hat, brushes, bucket filled with water, and a warm day.
THE PRINCESS AND THE PAINTER by Judith Bathie
A princess decides that painting castles is more enjoyable than looking pretty and playing with dolls. (WP)

JEWELER
Old jewelry, junk jewelry, macaroni, beads, glue, string, large-eyed needles, glitter, sequins and a work area.

MAIL CARRIER
Junk mail, stamp pads, Christmas stamps, a hat, badge, mail pouch (old shoulder strap purse).
MY MOTHER THE MAIL CARRIER by Inez Maury (FP) also in Spanish

MUSICIAN

Instruments and records from classical to jazz to folk rock. Homemade instruments: pot lids, wooden spoons, large empty cans, hair combs covered with wax paper, sand blocks made with sand paper and wood blocks, rice inside brown paper bags, etc.

TWO PIANO TUNERS by M.B. Goffstein
A young girl becomes adept at piano tuning.

PILOT

Jet pilot controls (c)
ANN CAN FLY by Frederick Phlegar
A young girl learns how to be a pilot.

POLICE OFFICER

Battery-powered traffic patrol cycle (cc)
Lego Police Set for preschoolers.

PRINTER

Paper and printing supplies, poster paint, ink pads, pencils, crayons for rubbings, cut fruit, gadgets, fingers, sponge shapes and work area.

SEA CAPTAIN

HURRAY FOR CAPTAIN JANE by Sam Reavin
An adventure story of Jane's fantasy about being the first female captain of an ocean liner.

THE MAGGIE B. by Irene Haas
Maggie cooks and cleans as well as steers and sings on her own ship.

SECRETARY

Toy phone, typewriter, paper, pencil, carbon paper, eraser, and a makeshift desk.

TRUCKER

Masking tape and toy trucks. An intricate freeway system can be layed out with masking tape on the kitchen floor.

VETERINARIAN

Stuffed animals, small boxes for beds and a doctor's kit.
WHAT CAN SHE BE: VETERINARIAN by Gloria and Esther Goldreich
Dr. Penny examines animals

GENERAL CAREER SKILL BOOKS

HE BEAR, SHE BEAR
 by Stan and Jan Berenstain
He and She bears exploring
things they BOTH can do...
build a house, knit a sock,
drive a train, make music
and messes.

BUSY PEOPLE AND HOW THEY DO THEIR WORK by Joe Kaufman
   Somewhat stereotyped, but generally has good non-sexist
   pictures of occupations AND girls and boys playing together.
WHO ARE THE PEOPLE IN YOUR NEIGHBORHOOD? A Sesame
   Street Pop-Up Book of a female mail carrier delivering
   mail to women and men in non-traditional jobs.
I CAN BE ANYTHING YOU CAN BE by Joel Rothman
   Multiethnic children "lightly" competing in the same
   occupations. Delightfully illustrated.
MOTHERS CAN DO ANYTHING by Joe Lasker
   Shows all kinds of interesting careers mothers can
   choose, including scientist and lion tamer.
MOMMIES AT WORK by Eve Merriam
   Mothers are shown in a wide variety of career
   choices while still functioning as mothers.

COLORING BOOKS

ABC WORKBOOK by Jean Mangi   Delightful, whimsical
   illustrations of non-traditional, non-sexist life options
   from Ann the Astronaut to Yolanda yelling yippee.
WHAT CAN WE BE? A COLORING BOOK FOR EVERYONE
This coloring book explains some of the training
   needed and the occupational demands of men
   and women in non-traditional jobs. Eleven of the
occupations discussed are men from Thomas, a private
corporate secretary, to Charlie, an airline steward.
(by Pamela Lechtman, American Association of University Women, Ventura, CA)

RESOURCES Career skill play kit materials can be used in combination with the following career skill resources to encourage exploring a variety of career choices.

BE WHAT YOU WANT TO BE by Phyllis and Noel Fiarotta A complete dress-up and pretend craft book. This book contains "how-to-make" props for 30 career choices from cash register, sewing machine to the kitchen sink. It is an excellent craft book for ADULTS to use to make role-playing props.

CHILDREN'S DICTIONARY OF OCCUPATIONS by William E. Hopke and Barbara M. Parramore. Over 300 untraditional occupations are defined.

- Plastic Hats (CC) Include crash helmet and goggles, cowperson hat, construction helmet, "straw" hat, derby, and firefighter's helmet.
- Occupational Puzzles (JP) Non-sexist, multiracial puzzles made of sturdy wood. See page 49.
- Robot Card Game (F) Non-sexist, multi-racial card game with male and female counterparts in various occupations. Similar to Old Maid.
- Scarecrow Card Game (WMCLC) Non-sexist card game
- My Mommy Is a Doctor (CBMC) Cassette or record of songs about women in non-traditional roles.
- Set of 8 photos of community jobs (FREE)
- Set of 8 photos of professional women (FREE)
- Community Helpers and Professional Women (CBMC) 16 black and white photos showing women in non-traditional jobs, such as of orthodontists, architects, milk women, surgeons, etc.
- Community Careers Flannelboard (I) 27 multiethnic women and men in work clothing.
- People at Work (I) 24 black and white photos of women and men at work.
- Our Community Helpers Play People (MB) 12 multi-racial stand-up figures of male and female workers.
- School Crossing Guard (CC) An occupational puzzle of a Black police officer.
- "Ranger" by Vickie Nelson (WMCLC) Poster of a female forest ranger.

Awakening Book Store
469 S. Bascom Ave.
San Jose, CA 95128

Women's Cultural Trust Bookstore
3601 Locust Walk
Philadelphia, PA 19174

Sojourner
1210 Pickens St.
Columbia, SC 29201

Something Ventured
524 S. Monroe St.
Green Bay, WI 54301

Cora: The Women's Bookmobile
342 Jarvis St.
Toronto, Ont., Canada

Vancouver Women's Bookstore
804 Richards St.
Vancouver, B.C., Canada

Sojourner Book Store
538 Redondo Ave.
Long Beach, CA 90814

Lilith
Fravenbuchladen GMBH
Kanstr. 125D
D-1000 Berlin 12, Germany

Ms. Atlas Press and Bookstore
120 E. San Carlos
San Jose, CA 95112

Womanspace
211½ N. 4th Ave.
Ann Arbor, MI 48108

Learn Me Bookstore
642 Grand Ave.
St. Paul, MI 55105

Womansplace
Dept. B 2401 N. 32nd St.
Phoenix, AZ 85008

Vesuvia
81 Johnson St.
Collingwood, Vic., Australia

The Feminist Bookshop
204 Rowe St.
Eastwood, NSW, Australia

The Oracle
1024 B St.
Hayward, CA 94541

Sisterhood Bookstore
1727 N. Spring St.
Los Angeles, CA 90012

Sisterhood Bookstore
1351 Westwood Blvd.
Los Angeles, CA 90024

A Woman's Place
5251 Broadway
Oakland, CA 94618

Women's Store
2965 Beech St.
San Diego, CA 92102

New Words Bookstore
419 Washington St.
Somerville, MA 02143

Amazon Book Store
2607 Hennepin Ave.
Minneapolis, MN 55401

New Earth Bookstore
24 E. 39 St.
Kansas City, MO 64111

Woman Books
201 W. 92nd St.
New York, NY 10025

A Woman's Place Bookstore
1300 S.W. Washington St.
Portland, OR 97302

Women's Cultural Trust
3601 Locust St.
Philadelphia, PA 19104

University Boulevard Bookstore
1728 Bissonett St.
Houston, TX 77005

It's About Time
5502 University Way N.E.
Seattle, WA 98105

A Room of One's Own
317 W. Johnson
Madison, WI 53703

Feminist Horizons
10586½ W. Pico Blvd.
Los Angeles, CA 90064

Page One
26 N. Lade St.
Pasadena, CA 91101

Bloodroot/Feminist Bookmobile
29 Hiawatha Ln.
Westport, CT 06880

Bloodroot
85 Ferris St.
Black Rock, Bridgeport, CT 06605

Herstore
112 E. Call St.
Tallahassee, FL 32301

Feminist Connection Bookshop
1202 W. Platt St.
Tampa, FL 33606

Our Place
12114 Knoll St.
Tampa, FL 33612

Her Shelf
2 Highland
Highland Park, MI 48203

The Woman's Eye
6344 S. Roseburg
St. Louis, MO 63105

The Book End
7641 Pacific St.
Omaha, NB 68114

Women's Concern Center
20 Main St.
Littleton, NH 03561

Sisterspace
1414 N. Broadway
Ft. Wayne, IN 46802

A Room of Her Own
3305 S. Peoria
Tulsa, OK 74105

Birmingham Booksellers
2222 E. Carson St.
Pittsburgh, PA 15203

ALLISON, LINDA, *Blood and Guts,* Boston: Little, Brown, 1976.

BERNABEI, RITA, "Can You Tell Me How to Get to Sesame Street?" mimeographed. Columbus, Ohio: Ohio State University, 1974.

BOOTH, ALAN, "Sex and Social Participation," *American Sociological Review,* April, 1972: pp. 183–93.

CHAVETZ, JANET SALTZMAN, *Masculine/Feminine or Human?* Illinois: F. E. Peacock Publishers, Inc. 1974.

COOPER, JANE, *Love at First Bite,* New York: Knopf, 1977.

DODSON, FITZHUGH, *How to Parent,* New York: New American Library, 1970.

DUNN, RITA and KENNETH DUNN, *How to Raise Independent and Professionally Successful Daughters,* Englewood Cliffs, N.J.: Prentice-Hall, 1977.

EPSTEIN, CYNTHIA FUCHS, *Woman's Place,* Berkeley, Calif.: University of California Press, 1970.

FREEMAN, JO, "The Origins of the Women's Liberation Movement," *American Journal of Sociology,* vol. 78, no. 4, 1973, pp. 792–811.

GERSHUNG, H. LEE, "Sexist Semantics in the Dictionary," *A Review of General Semantics,* vol. XXXI, no. 2, (June 1974), pp. 159–68.

GOODMAN, LOUIS WOLF and JANET LEVER, reported on in "A Report on Children's Toys" from Ms. Magazine in *And Jill Came Tumbling After: Sexism in American Education,* ed. Judith Stacey, et al., New York: Dell Publishing Co., 1974.

GUTTENTAG, MARCIA and HELEN BRAY, *Undoing Sex Stereotypes,* New York: McGraw-Hill, 1976.

HARTLEY, RUTH E., "Sex Role Pressures and the Socialization of the Male Child," in *Men and Masculinity,* ed. Joseph Pleck and Jack Sawyer, Englewood Cliffs, New Jersey: Prentice-Hall, 1974.

HARWOOD, JOLEEN, et al., *Survey of Sex-Role Stereotypes in Preschool,* Utah: Utah University, 1975.

HELSON, R., "Childhood Interests Related to Creativity in Women," *Journal of Consulting Psychology,* 29, 1965.

HYDE, JANET and BENJAMIN ROSENBERG, "What Are Little Girls Made of?" in Newsline Section, *Psychology Today,* August 1974, p. 43+.

KAGAN, JEROME, "On the Meaning of Behavior: Illustrations from the Infant," *Child Development,* 40, (1969), pp. 1121–1134.

KOHLBERG, L., "A Cognitive-Developmental Analysis of Children's Sex Role Concepts and Attitudes," in *The Development of Sex Differences,* ed., Maccoby, Eleanor, Stanford: Stanford University Press, 1966.

LOOFT, WILLIAM R., "Sex Differences in the Expression of Vocational Aspirations by Elementary School Children," *Developmental Psychology,* (September, 1971), p. 366.

LOVE, KEITH, ". . . House Wife's Value Adds Up," *New York Times News Service,* 1976.

MACCOBY, ELEANOR and CAROL JACKLIN, *The Psychology of Sex Differences,* Stanford: Stanford University Press, 1974.

MEAD, MARGARET, *Sex and Temperament in Three Primitive Societies,* New York: Dell Publishing Co., 1969 (first published in 1935).

MILES, BETTY, *Save the Earth,* New York: Knopf, 1974.

MONEY, JOHN and ANKE A. EHRHARDT, "Rearing of a Sex-reassigned Normal Male Infant after Traumatic Loss of the Penis," in *Sex: Male/Gender: Masculine,* ed., Jack Petras, New York: Alfred Publishing Co., 1975.

MOORE, JUDY and ERIC CHARLTON, study reported in *Masculine/Feminine or Human?,* Janet Saltzman Chafetz, Illinois: F. E. Peacock Publishers, Inc., 1974, pp. 82–83.

Ms. Magazine article, "A Report on Children's Toys" in *And Jill Came Tumbling After: Sexism in American Education,* ed. Stacey, Judith, et al., New York: Dell Publishing Co., 1974.

NASH, SHARON CHURNIM, a brief report in *Intellect,* 103, (April, 1975), pp. 424–25.

Newsweek article, "What TV Does to Kids," *Newsweek,* (Feb. 21, 1977), pp. 63+.

Pact Guidelines, Public Action: Coalition of Toys, 38 West 9th Street, New York, N.Y. 10011, 1977.

RARICK, G. L., "Competitive Sports for Girls: Effects on Growth, Development, and General Health," *Education for Survival: Schools and Sex Role Stereotypes,* October, 1972.

Re:act: Action for Children's Television News Magazine, ACT, Spring 1978, vol. 7, no. 3.

RHEINGOLD, H.L. and K. V. COOK, "Contents of Boys' and Girls' Rooms as an Index of Parents' Behavior, *Child Development,* vol. 46, 1975, pp. 459–463.

ROSSI, ALICE, "Equality between the Sexes," in *The Woman in America,* ed. Robert Jay Lifton, Boston: Houghton-Mifflin, 1964.

RUBIN, JEFFREY Z. et al., "The Eye of the Beholder: Parents' Views on Sex of Newborns," *American Journal of Orthopsychiatry,* Vol. 44, no. 4, 1974.

SCOTT, ANNE CRITTENDEN, "The Values of Housework," *Ms.* (July, 1972), pp. 56–59.

SCOTT, ANNE CRITTENDEN, "Closing the Muscle Gap," *Ms.* (September, 1974), pp. 49–55.

STOLLER, R. J., "Effects of Parents' Attitudes on Core Gender Identity," *International Journal of Psychiatry,* 4, (1967), p. 57.

SUTTON-SMITH, BRIAN, "Child's Play," *Psychology Today,* (December, 1971), p. 67+.

Toy Manufacturers of America Quote reported on in "Gifts for Free Children," *Ms.,* by Letty Cottin Pogrebin, December, 1976.

U. S. Department of Labor, Women's Bureau, Washington, D.C., 1974, 1975.

VEITCH, BEVERLY, THELMA HARMS, TIA WALLACE, and GERRY WALLACE, *A Child's Cookbook,* 656 Terra California Drive, #3, Walnut Creek, CA 94595.

VOGEL, SUSAN, et al., *Sesame Street and Sex-Role Stereotypes,* Pittsburgh, Pa.: KNOW, 1970.

WEITZMAN, LENORE, et al., "Sex-Role Socialization in Picture Books for Preschool Children," *American Journal of Sociology,* Vol. 77, No. 6 (May, 1972), pp. 1125–1150.

and, now it's your turn.

We'd like to hear your reactions AND we'd like to know about other resources and activities you'd like us to include in our next edition of GUE.

1. CUT page along dotted line (‒‒‒‒‒).
2. WRITE suggestions on the back side of this page.
3. FOLD along dotted lines (..........).
4. PASTE, STAPLE, GLUE or TAPE closed.
5. AFFIX STAMP.
6. PAT yourself on the back.
7. THANK YOU.

FOLD

FOLD

POSTAGE US ¢

GROWING UP EQUAL
P.O. BOX 266
SURFSIDE, CA 90743

write on

BETTER FOR BOTH